Tim Dedopulos

WIZARDS

THIS IS A CARLTON BOOK

Text and design copyright © 2001 Carlton Books Limited

This edition published by Carlton Books Limited 2001
20 Mortimer Street
London
W!T 3 JW

A CIP catalogue for this book is available from the British Library.

Art Editor Adam Wright
Design Mary Ryan
Picture Research Faye Parish
Production Janette Davis

ISBN 1 84222 433 6 (U.S: 1 84222 488 3)

Printed in Italy

Tim Dedopulos

WIZARDS

a magical history tour

CARLTON
BOOKS

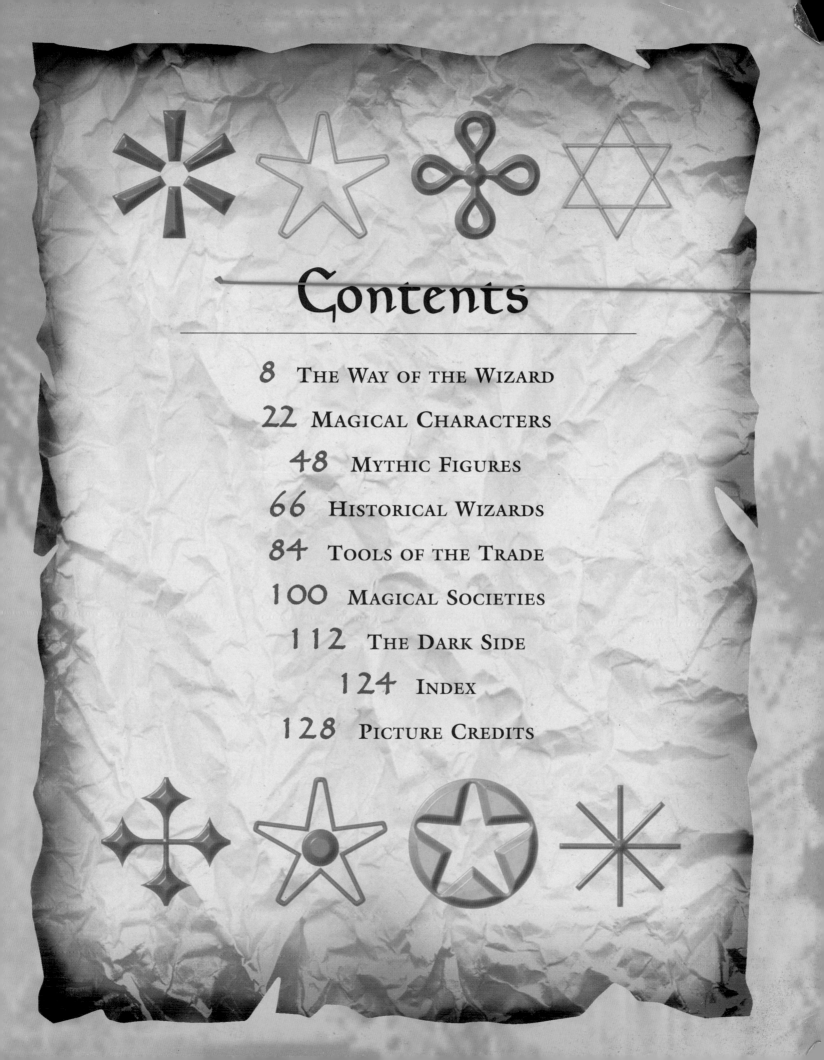

Contents

The Way of the Wizard

1

The Way of the Wizard

An Introduction to Wizardry

Wizards are dangerous and mysterious. They have mighty powers, casting spells with nothing more than a gesture and a word or conducting elaborate rituals that produce hidden results. They control the forces of the world but often stand back from it, alone and withdrawn. They are the ultimate image of mankind's desire to control his surroundings – willpower and wisdom made human.

An Introduction to Wizardry

Magic is as old as thought. It comes from the same ideas that created the earliest beginnings of religion in the minds of our earliest ancestors – the destructive power of fire, the awesome displays of fierce weather, or the exceptional luck in the hunt. It is fascinating to imagine that the forces of the universe can be controlled with either a thought or a word. Many of us would love to live in a world – a mysterious and exciting world hidden behind ours, that can reach out and save us – where men and women of power can perform such supernatural marvels ... It's a tempting idea.

Of course, even within the world of the wizard, only a very special few have the potential to master the forces of magic. It takes willpower, intelligence, persistent effort and solid belief. If everyone could learn, then everyone would – wizards are rare, and that means that it is difficult to become one. Fictional and mythological wizards are usually born that way, with the power buried within. Harry Potter is a wizard by birth, and magic runs in his blood. Merlin, King Arthur's wizard, is not entirely human, and gets his power from elsewhere. Gandalf from *The Lord of the Rings* is a heavenly being in disguise. Luke and Anakin in *Star Wars*, Garion in the *Belgariad*, Will Stanton in *The Dark is Rising*, Rand in *The Wheel of Time* ... over and over again, wizards are born to their power and grow up knowing nothing about it until it bursts out of them.

Wizards are usually thought of as crotchety old men wearing robes and pointy hats. That isn't always true, though. Wizardry goes beyond any simple description, and it isn't only found in fantasy – you also find it in modern fictional settings, in science fiction, in mythology, and in all sorts of other places.

✦ Far Left: A medieval wizard uses Heaven to subdue Hell.

✦ Left: The ghost of a dead woman is called back to life by a wizard.

There are even real historical people who have claimed to be wizards. There are no stereotypes that you can rely on. Circe of Greek myth and Baba Yaga of Russian folklore are female wizards, Harry Potter is a child (and Hermione, his friend, is a girl too), John Dee really lived in the sixteenth century, Rincewind, the Discworld wizard, only knows one spell, and Jedi Master Yoda isn't even slightly human.

In this book, we are going to take a detailed look at the world of wizards and wizardry. We will investigate all of the most famous wizards, both fictional and historical. That includes information about their lives, magical powers, interests and the worlds (or times) in which they lived. We will also look at the items and assistants with which wizards surround themselves, the places they like to live in, the organizations that they belong to, and the tools that they use in their magical work. First of all, though, we are going to consider what being a wizard actually means, how you can tell wizards from other types of magic-using people, and the different varieties of wizard that you might come across.

The Nature of Magic

The most important requirement for being a wizard is the ability to use magic. Without it a wizard is nothing much more than a stage magician. Magic is at the heart of a wizard's powers, but it manifests itself in many different forms, and may come from many different places. It is important to know what magic really is. Magic is the art of causing something to happen without going through the normal process that is required to make it happen. Everything that happens normally involves a chain of events, each leading from one to the next on the way to the result. That is called "causality", because each moment is physically caused by the one that happened before it. Magic cuts straight through that, providing you with a more direct way to achieve the result.

The science fiction writer Arthur C. Clarke once said that: *"In a sufficiently advanced society, technology is indistinguishable from magic."* He meant that if our science was good enough, we would be able to achieve seemingly magical results. That may be true, but it misses the point entirely. Magic is about causing effects by the power of your mind alone. If you use technology, you are not a wizard – you are a scientist.

Let's look at an example of that. Moving from place to place normally requires you to somehow travel from A to B. You have to use energy to move, or someone or something else – like a horse, a car or a plane – has to use energy to carry you. Wizardry could move you from A to B without energy being used. That is not possible in normal causality ... and that is what makes it magic. If you use a scientific teleport device, there is a causal explanation – and an energy source – so it's normal causality, not magic.

✦ Right: A real wizard has no need for an audience ...

✦ Far Right: ... while a stage magician has to look flashy and mysterious.

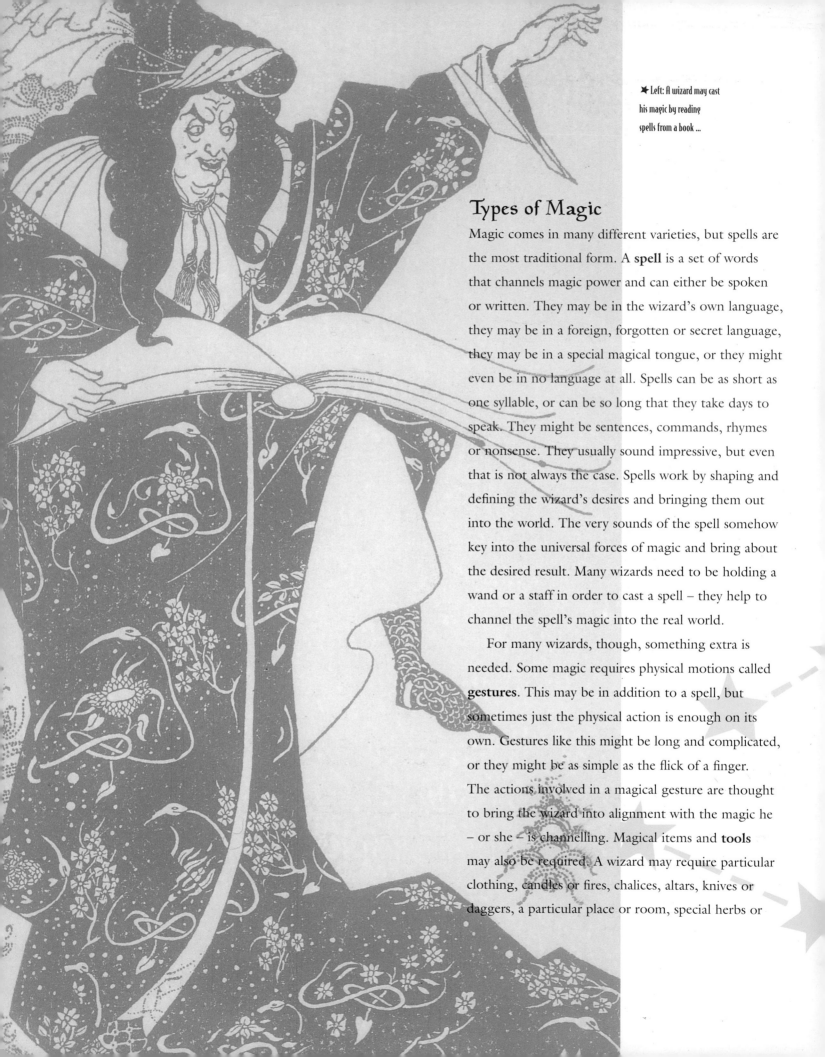

✦ Left: A wizard may cast
his magic by reading
spells from a book ...

Types of Magic

Magic comes in many different varieties, but spells are
the most traditional form. A **spell** is a set of words
that channels magic power and can either be spoken
or written. They may be in the wizard's own language,
they may be in a foreign, forgotten or secret language,
they may be in a special magical tongue, or they might
even be in no language at all. Spells can be as short as
one syllable, or can be so long that they take days to
speak. They might be sentences, commands, rhymes
or nonsense. They usually sound impressive, but even
that is not always the case. Spells work by shaping and
defining the wizard's desires and bringing them out
into the world. The very sounds of the spell somehow
key into the universal forces of magic and bring about
the desired result. Many wizards need to be holding a
wand or a staff in order to cast a spell – they help to
channel the spell's magic into the real world.

For many wizards, though, something extra is
needed. Some magic requires physical motions called
gestures. This may be in addition to a spell, but
sometimes just the physical action is enough on its
own. Gestures like this might be long and complicated,
or they might be as simple as the flick of a finger.
The actions involved in a magical gesture are thought
to bring the wizard into alignment with the magic he
– or she – is channelling. Magical items and **tools**
may also be required. A wizard may require particular
clothing, candles or fires, chalices, altars, knives or
daggers, a particular place or room, special herbs or

✦ Left: ... or may need special ingredients such as morning dew.

place in a special or magical location – a lonely hilltop, an underground temple, a forest glade – and require a number of different tools. They can get extremely complicated, and are usually ruined if they are disturbed. For that reason, most wizards prefer simpler spells when they are available.

Most magical effects fall into one of five different categories. Spells that change one thing into another, or change part of something, are spells of **transformation**. Typical transformation spells include changing lead into gold, turning an enemy into a toad, or shifting your appearance to look and sound like someone else. When something is summoned from another place or created out of thin air, the process is called **invocation**. This can include calling servants, creatures or monsters from other dimensions, casting a fireball at a rival, or cloaking yourself in an illusion. When feelings, emotions and other intangibles are changed or manipulated, it is known as **evocation**. This covers things like love spells, making people avoid a certain area, stopping time, or cursing someone to bad luck. Playing around with physical qualities – location, speed, weight, size, health and so on – falls under **manipulation**. This includes teleporting and moving objects around as well as curing disease or becoming invisible. Finally, **divination** deals with spells that look into other times and places, or ones that seek answers. This can involve making predictions, discovering who last held an object, learning someone's history, or spying on a distant place.

other magical substances, bells or instruments, assistants or sacrifices, or all sorts of other things. These are collectively known as tools, even though an assistant is a living being, and wands and staffs are so ubiquitous that they don't count.

A **ritual** is a piece of magic that requires one or more tools. Most rituals include spells, and often gestures as well. Rituals are as variable as everything else and may take months or just a moment to complete, but most last for an hour or two. They usually take

Other Wizardly Powers

There is more to being a wizard than just magic, however. There are a number of powers and abilities that wizards often possess that are magical, but do not really count as a spell that can be cast. These may be passive abilities that are always active for the wizard even if he or she is doing something else, or they may be specific skills that the wizard can use when he or she wants to. They are differentiated from spells in that they do not necessarily have a specific result – a spell makes something happen; other powers, on the other hand, may just be.

✦ Above Right: A wizard's ritual is far more impressive on the astral plane.

✦ Right: The Oracle of Delphi could predict the future.

Psychic ability is a good example. Many wizards are psychic in one way or another. They may get spontaneous glimpses of the future – unasked for, unexplained and sometimes even irrelevant. This can also manifest itself as knowing when they are in danger. Others can read minds or emotions, or at least feel the presence of other beings around them. A few can even tell which actions are going to give the best results, or even when something is going to prove to be a mistake. The Jedi's mind-control ability, for example, is a spell that requires a gesture to cause a result – the Jedi gestures and tells the victim what to think – but their power of perceiving surroundings through the Force is a psychic ability, because it is like a sixth sense, and it is always on. Some wizards have just one psychic ability, but others may have a whole range of different psychic senses and powers.

Astral projection is similar to psychic ability, but there are certain differences. It is a power that allows a wizard to step out of his or her physical body into an invisible shell of consciousness. This shell can then go to other locations at the speed of thought, and perhaps even to other times or dimensions. When in an astral form, most wizards can watch and listen passively, but can take no physical action. A few can cast spells from the astral shell, which makes them immensely powerful.

Some wizards are partly **immortal** in one way or another. This is usually limited. The wizard may be immune to ageing and disease but not to injury or attack – or vice versa. Even fully immortal wizards usually have one weakness or vulnerability that can be used to harm them, in the same way that a werewolf can only be harmed by silver. Ageless wizards mostly look old, but as always there are exceptions, and some

immortals may appear young, even child-like. Similarly, a frail old wizard may well prove completely invulnerable to physical harm. There are even some wizards who regularly change their appearance, altering their apparent age, sex, country of origin and even species on a whim. Some go so far that they even forget what they originally looked like.

One of the greatest wizardly powers, however, is **knowledge**. Most wizards are well learned, with access to all sorts of information that those around them do not have. The term "wizard" itself comes from the derivative "wise". Often, a wizard will have a knowledge of certain chemical or physical processes that give him access to entirely natural powers – how to mix explosive powders, for example, or which herbs can be used to promote natural healing.

In the hands of someone intelligent and dedicated, almost any knowledge can be a powerful tool or weapon, whether it is the knowledge to bring about magical changes in the world, or the knowledge to bring about physical changes. To the unenlightened, there may seem to be no difference between the two – what does it matter if the wizard mixes two powders or waves a wand, if a ball of fire is the result? Sometimes, a wizard may be a scientist as well.

✱ Below: Virgil's great knowledge gave him a reputation as a sorcerer.

Masters of Magic

Wizards are not the only people with access to the forces of magic. Although a wizard needs some sort of access to magical abilities to be a wizard, the reverse doesn't automatically hold true – having access to magic does not automatically make you a wizard. In fact, it is really all a matter of style. Wizards impose their will on reality and force it to conform to their spells and rituals. Other types of magically empowered people approach the universe in a rather different way, particularly witches, shamans and mystics.

✦ Right: Witches are in touch with nature and work with it.

It is common to assume that wizards and **witches** are just male and female versions of the same thing, for example. The pointy hats that they both wear go a long way to making that an obvious assumption. It is not actually correct, though. The Harry Potter books aside, witches are not female wizards. Although most wizards are men and most witches are women, they approach magic – and the rest of life – in very different ways. Witches work with nature and the spirits of the earth. Their magic comes from long rituals that usually have several participants, and it works by summoning, persuading or controlling natural spirits and energies. Old wisdom – herb lore, the power of fire, knots and candles, minor curses and cures, the rhythm of the cycles and the natural times of power – forms the basis of their power, which is useful for everyday things. A witch can tell your future, make someone fall in love with you, dry up your cows, or go flying on a broomstick. A lot of witches' magic has to be done at specific times or in specific places: when the moon is full; at midnight on a Friday; naked around a bonfire; in a sacred grove at dawn; and so on. If you want to strike a bargain with the spirit of a forest, learn the future or have an enemy become ill and die, you need to go to a witch. The correct term for a male witch is a warlock (according to historical definitions); the correct term for a female wizard is actually still a wizard.

A **shaman** is another nature-based spell-caster. Unlike witches, shamen work alone, usually on behalf of one tribe or village. Their power comes from being able to access a special realm where spirits live, using a power a bit like astral projection. The first time a shaman enters the spirit world, he or she is adopted by one of a number of powerful spirits called totems. These totems usually represent a certain species of animal, and are named after it – Bear is strong and slow to anger; Raven is clever; and Spider is wise and patient. A shaman's totem reflects his or her true personality. Different parts of the world have different totem animals, but almost any living species can have a totem. Once the shaman has been accepted by the totem, the spirit realm is open. The totem acts as protector, guide and teacher. The shaman can read the future by calling on the totem to guide a particular type of divination, and can heal the sick by journeying into the spirit realm and correcting whatever is wrong with the patient's soul. He or she can also tell the village's hunters where to find food, and advise the chief on the things that are going to be important to the people.

Mystics gain access to magical powers through physical and mental exercises. These exercises are often extremely difficult, dangerous or uncomfortable, and it can take years and years of work to start gaining powers. Mystics normally have control over their own bodies, and also acquire a range of impressive psychic powers, but rarely have any skill at directly influencing others. Common feats include being able to slow ageing and stop disease, ignore poisons, the ability to harden the body to resist weapons or punch through stone, holding their breath for days on end, becoming blindingly fast in combat, or climbing seemingly impossible surfaces – all of which would be immensely dangerous tricks without magical powers. Some mystics are peaceful, and focus their powers into mental abilities and passive skills, while others, like the legendary monks of China's Shaolin temple, are devastatingly dangerous martial artists.

Magical powers can be found with other types of person as well. **Demigods** are the mightiest of heroes and villains, either the child of a union between a god and a mortal, or a fraction of a larger god crammed into a human form. Their powers are a natural result of their

✦ Left: Mystics may be able to look out to other places and times for clients.

✦ Below: A shaman's ritual may involve the whole tribe in a frenzied dance.

divine blood, and need no spell or concentration to activate. Their abilities, while often spell-like, are not linked to magic in any way, and they dedicate themselves to furthering their divine interests. **Occultists** are normal humans who use complicated traditional spells and rituals to bring about fairly minor effects, such as luck in business or gambling, or to heighten someone's affection. Magic is not natural, instinctive or a core part of identity for an occultist; it's more like a job or a hobby. Some of the legendary occult rituals offer incredible abilities – the power to become invisible, to change shape, or to control the mind of another person – but many of these rituals are long lost. There are lots of types of occultist, and many people actually try using occultism to solve their problems.

Different Strokes

Just as there many types of people with access to magical powers who are not wizards, there are also several different categories that wizards can fall into. Different spell-casters have different interests, or channel their abilities into separate lines. They all share the common ground of wizardry – using the power of magic to force reality into doing unnatural or unusual things – but they have different skills. Some are so specialized that they cannot do anything outside of one narrow field, while for others, their specialization is more a question of style than of actual ability.

The main division of wizarding style is between sorcerers and ritualists. **Sorcerers** are wizards who use their powers almost spontaneously, with no ritual and almost nothing in the way of spell or gesture. Their magic tends to be strong, sudden and showy, rather than subtle or gradual. Sorcerers tend to be good at invocation and manipulation. If a wizard is frequently using magic without actually speaking a spell, or spends a lot of time on flashy magic such as casting fireballs, collapsing walls, flying or changing shape, he or she is likely to be a sorcerer. Sorcerers often neglect the usual trappings of wizardly life, and may appear to be a completely normal person, perhaps not even carrying a wand or staff. Despite the staff he carries, Gandalf is a typical sorcerer.

Ritualists are the opposite. These are the wizards who wear robes and hats, carry wands, and devote time and energy to each spell that they cast. Their powers are less immediate than those of sorcerers, but they make up for it in other ways. Ritual wizards can only cast spells that they know while some sorcerers can make it up as they go along. On the other hand, a ritualist's spell can create extremely complicated results, and may have several subtle, long-lasting effects. It takes a ritual to create a portable

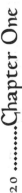

✦ Right: A ritualist in his underground temple, preparing a spell.

manor house, filled with lavish rooms, dedicated servants and delicious foodstuffs, in which you can accommodate 20 people overnight when you are travelling and still fold up to the size of a matchbox and put in your pocket the next morning. For complex stuff, ritual is a must. Ritualists are particularly good at evocation and divination. Harry Potter is a ritualist, although most of his rituals are quite short.

There are various kinds of wizard who specialize in certain areas, known as **domains**. **Necromancers** specialize in the dead. They can create zombies, skeletons and other undead, talk to people who have passed away, predict the future or learn about the past, and use magic to destroy things and kill people. **Alchemists** work with equipment and ritual to create transformations, turning one thing into another. Their traditional aims are to turn lead into gold, and to gain eternal life.

Demonologists are skilled at summoning and controlling demons and other powerful beings. Their power usually consists of commanding other beings to perform magical acts for them, and they may actually be powerless away from their

magical slaves. Demonologists and necromancers are usually evil. **Elementalists** specialize in the control and manipulation of one or more physical substances. These are often the Greek classical elements of air, fire, water and earth, but can also be Chinese elements such as wood, stone or metal, or just about any other broad class of substance. Elementalists can make their particular elements do just about anything, and can often summon their element as well – a water wizard could make it rain, part the sea, breathe water, or make a lake lash out at a boat. **High Mages**, finally, are concerned with the universe as a whole. Their magic is abstract and difficult to understand, and often relates to other magic, or to the balance of good and evil in the world. They can be immensely powerful, but do not usually stoop to interfere in day-to-day affairs.

MAGICAL CHARACTERS 2

Magical Characters

Famous Fictional Wizards

Wizards become famous. It's almost inevitable. As their power grows, word of their incredible achievements spreads across the land. Whispers, rumours and travellers' tales combine to form legends, and the legends in turn become bedside stories. Sometimes the telling inflates the truth, and the wizard may find that his skill is dwarfed by his reputation. On other occasions, certain feats might be overlooked as too amazing to be true. Even reclusive wizards may still become known, their names attached to wild rumours by suspicious locals. Learning magic takes time and practice and most wizards are old, so it is amazing that the most famous of them all is a boy.

harry Potter

The creation of author J.K. Rowling, Harry Potter is the world's best-known wizard. From the moment he first appeared in 1997, his adventures have been thrilling fans all over the globe. With his award-winning books selling tens of millions of copies and a major Hollywood blockbuster backing him up, Harry's is the most prominent name in all of wizarding. His beginnings were humble, though.

BIOGRAPhY: Harry Potter is an orphan. His parents, James and Lily Potter, were murdered while he was still a baby. Their killer was the evil Lord Voldemort, mightiest of the Dark wizards. Voldemort tried to kill Harry as well, but special protections around the infant bounced the attack back at him. Voldemort was left dreadfully crippled, and Harry received a vivid scar on his forehead in the shape of a lightning bolt.

After the attack, Harry was given into the care of his aunt and uncle, Vernon and Petulia Dursley and their son, Dudley. Aggressively anti-wizard and resentful of the imposition, the Dursleys treated Harry appallingly, more like a slave than a family member. He grew up knowing next to nothing of his parents or even about magic. That all changed when he was invited to enrol at Hogwarts' School of Wizardry. He suddenly discovered the wizarding world, and found out that he was a celebrity, famed for surviving the evil Voldemort's attack.

Since that time, Harry has had several daring adventures with his friends Ron Weasley and Hermione Granger. In addition to being brave, resourceful and resilient, Harry is an excellent Quidditch player, his amazing broomstick control giving him a big edge in the frenetic airborne sport.

✦ Far Left: Berlin fans celebrate Harry Potter.

✦ Left: The movie world's face of Harry.

✦ Below: Joanne Rowling, Harry's creator.

WORLD: In Harry's topsy-turvy version of Earth, wizards keep themselves very carefully separated from non-magical people, whom they refer to as "muggles". Wizardly activities are restricted so as to not risk alarming the general population, and most of the community lives inside magical areas that are invisible to muggles. Hogwarts School, with its towers, cellars, Great Hall and stone corridors, is an extremely magical place – so much so that even technology stops

✦ Below: All sorts of Harry Potter merchandise is available ...

✦ Bottom: ... but nothing beats the books themselves.

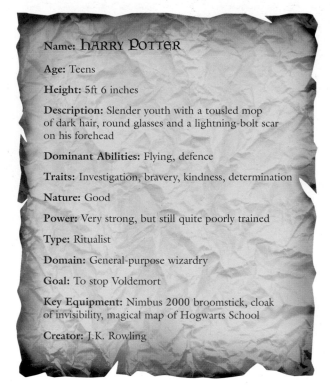

Name: HARRY POTTER

Age: Teens

Height: 5ft 6 inches

Description: Slender youth with a tousled mop of dark hair, round glasses and a lightning-bolt scar on his forehead

Dominant Abilities: Flying, defence

Traits: Investigation, bravery, kindness, determination

Nature: Good

Power: Very strong, but still quite poorly trained

Type: Ritualist

Domain: General-purpose wizardry

Goal: To stop Voldemort

Key Equipment: Nimbus 2000 broomstick, cloak of invisibility, magical map of Hogwarts School

Creator: J.K. Rowling

working within its boundaries. The headmaster, Albus Dumbledore, is an immensely powerful wizard, and a staunch ally of Harry's.

Throughout the books, wizardry is a hidden world, tucked just around the corner from mundane reality. Diagon Alley, a major shopping street for wizards, is located in London, but hidden behind an innocuous door. Platform 9¾, on King's Cross station, can only be reached by running through a solid barrier. The wizards themselves do all they can to keep hidden from the muggle world, and in fact have very little understanding of it.

As Hogwarts is a boarding school, Harry spends most of his time within its grounds. Each of the four Houses has its own tower, and rivalry for the annual House Trophy is as fierce as it is for the Quidditch Cup. The sinister house of Slytherin is famous for producing Dark wizards – Harry, naturally, belongs to

brave Gryffindor. The teachers and other adult figures never quite seem to know what's going on, with the exception of wise old Dumbledore, who always turns out to have known everything all along, so Harry and his friends are repeatedly left to thwart Voldemort's evil plans on their own.

MAGIC: Spells are activated by a short, pig-Latin invocation (*"Expecto Patronum"* for example), and require the use of a wand. Once out of the school system, wizards seek jobs in a number of different magical areas, and enjoy status according to career, wealth and family, much like the rest of us. Female wizards share an equal footing. Although they are sometimes referred to as "witches" in the books, they practise wizardry, not witchcraft. Wizards have wands and hats and blast things with spells, while witches have bonfires and nakedness, and conduct night-time rituals in secluded glades. Female wizards are a long-standing tradition, and the term should really be thought of as gender-neutral.

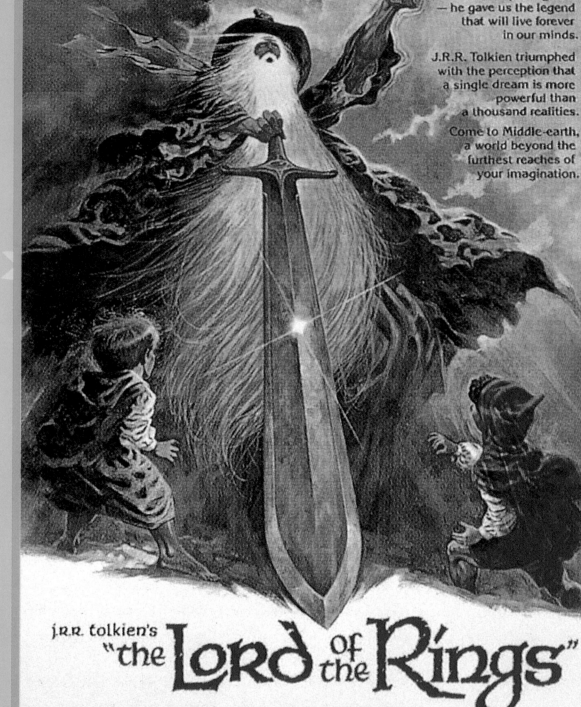

► Right: Gandalf the Grey is at the heart of *The Lord of the Rings.*

Gandalf

The Lord of the Rings, by J.R.R. Tolkein, is the book that created the entire fantasy genre. It has been consistently voted the best book of the twentieth century in reader's poll after reader's poll, and it is certainly one of the most influential. The genre of books that followed it is the second most popular on the planet (after romantic fiction, in case you were wondering). Its patterns and settings have become almost regulation for most works in the fantasy field. Gandalf himself strides through the book, a mighty and mysterious central figure with incredible powers tempered by near-infinite kindness and wisdom. In many ways, Gandalf is the archetypal wizard – the one who defines all the others.

BIOGRAPHY: Ancient and timeless, Gandalf is not actually human. Like the other Istari – the wizards of Middle Earth, the land that *The Lord of the Rings* is set in – he is one of the Maya, a spiritual being working for the forces of goodness, clothed in human form and mind. He is an old man with long white hair and a long white beard, dressed in robes and a mantle. He carries a staff that is the channel for his power, and also wears the Red Ring of Fire, a magical ring of incredible power that gives him command over flame and can kindle passions and miracles.

Gandalf has held a number of names over the centuries. His original name was Olórin, and he is known as Mithrandir by the elves. He arrived in Middle Earth during the Third Age, when Sauron, the ancient enemy, was starting to re-establish himself in the forest called Greenwood the Great. As Sauron's power grew, and Greenwood came to be known as Mirkwood, Gandalf and the other Istari came out of the west by boat. Gandalf had many powers of mind and hand, and travelled through Middle Earth talking to humans and elves, as well as to the animals and birds, gathering information.

Gandalf was the most vigilant of all the wizards, and suspected that the darkness in Mirkwood was due to Sauron regaining his powers. He drove the darkness out of the forest, but it returned, slowly. Gandalf went there again, came face to face with Sauron, and managed to escape with his life. He tried to persuade a council of the leaders of the free people to act against the enemy, but was stalled by the traitorous wizard who led the council, Saruman. Finally, it became obvious that action was necessary and Saruman could delay no longer, and Sauron was driven out of Mirkwood again. The enemy had regained his former powers, however, and fell back to his old kingdom of Mordor.

In the battles that followed, Gandalf's wisdom and power tipped the balance in favour of the free people. Saruman the traitor was cast down, and Sauron was destroyed for once and for all. With his work done, Gandalf left Middle Earth as he had come, by boat, and returned to the ancient lands of the west.

WORLD: In many ways, the land of Middle Earth itself is the real hero of Tolkein's opus. He saw his works as a history of what could have been rather than seeing himself as a writer of an epic adventure story, and he often paid as much attention to the world and its past as he did to the characters and plots. As a result, the history, geography and politics of Middle Earth are well known.

Middle Earth is a magical place. It is populated by a number of sentient species, the "Free Peoples" – humans, elves, dwarves and halflings – as well as several other species of intelligent creatures, ranging from fairly pleasant beings such as ents to evil monsters like orcs, half-orcs, trolls, giants and dragons. The Free Peoples are settled in a number of nations and regions. Humans occupy a number of different countries, and elves, dwarves and halflings all have various nations, enclaves and territories. Some of the monstrous species – most notably the orcs of Mordor – also have their own national areas. Middle Earth itself is not unlike Europe or America. It is large and mostly temperate in climate, with great mountains, huge plains, pleasant dales and vast tracts of forest hiding strange and ancient creatures. To the north, the land becomes steadily more polar, getting colder and bleaker; to the south, it becomes hot and sandy.

Magic is a common companion in Middle Earth. Although Gandalf and his fellow Istari are the only ones formally known as wizards, many elves also have access to magical abilities, and rare individuals of the other species also possess power. In addition, many

magical objects and items exist that can grant special abilities. The sword "Sting", for example, passed by Bilbo the hobbit to his nephew Frodo, has the power to glow with blue fire when orcs are nearby. The rings of power – three for the elves (including Gandalf's Red Ring), seven for the dwarves, nine for the humans, and one master control ring – are at the other end of the power scale, and are able to grant incredible powers. For most of the population, monsters, sorcery and the undead are things to be cautious

✦ Right: Galadriel, the elves' queen, was a potent sorceress in her own right.

Chapter Two

30 ·········

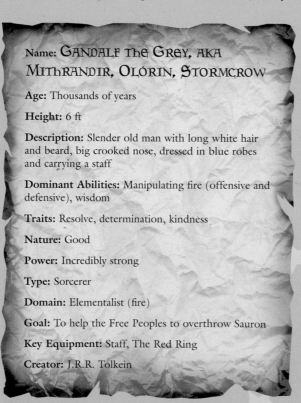

Name: GANDALF THE GREY, AKA MITHRANDIR, OLÓRIN, STORMCROW

Age: Thousands of years

Height: 6 ft

Description: Slender old man with long white hair and beard, big crooked nose, dressed in blue robes and carrying a staff

Dominant Abilities: Manipulating fire (offensive and defensive), wisdom

Traits: Resolve, determination, kindness

Nature: Good

Power: Incredibly strong

Type: Sorcerer

Domain: Elementalist (fire)

Goal: To help the Free Peoples to overthrow Sauron

Key Equipment: Staff, The Red Ring

Creator: J.R.R. Tolkein

of, rather than merely being a part of legend and rumour.

MAGIC: Gandalf is largely sorcerous in his use of power, leaving ritual aside. He is a mighty wizard, with huge reserves of strength and wisdom, and the knowledge to back it up and apply it. He is a particular master of fire, with a love of creating incredible firework displays. Although he rarely bothers with speaking spells, he can call upon them when required. Others in Middle Earth are more ritual-dependent. Tom Bombadil relies on – and responds to – spells; the elves tend to draw on long-established rituals to construct wondrous artefacts.

Yoda

A wizened little old alien whose comical appearance hides incredible power and wisdom, Yoda is one of the rarest of wizardly breeds – a science-fiction wizard. The original *Star Wars* films imprinted themselves on an entire generation who were thrilled by the blend of high-tech special effects, spaghetti western plots and fantasy-style magic and mysticism. The *Star Wars* series was created and conceived by producer-director George Lucas, and Hollywood found the whole idea so peculiar that it took him ten years to raise the money to produce the first one. Yoda belongs mainly to the second film of the original trilogy, *The Empire Strikes Back*. He has proved so popular, however, that he has featured in every *Star Wars* film since.

BIOGRAPHY: A mighty master of the Jedi religion and the being responsible for training new Jedi, Yoda was a powerful individual, both politically and spiritually. A senior member of the Jedi council in the old Republic, he was already more than 850 years old when he escaped the destruction of the Jedi at the hands of a traitor and fled to the jungle world of Dagobah. By using the planet's natural, dark emanations as covering camouflage, he managed to stay hidden from his enemies for more than 20 years.

In due time, Yoda's old friend and pupil, Obi-Wan Kenobi, managed to get Luke Skywalker to go to Dagobah. When he got there, Yoda took on the role of trainer one last time, and did his best to nurture the power inside the young man. Luke progressed rapidly

✦ Far left: Don't be fooled – Yoda may be sci-fi but he's still a wizard.

✦ Left: Master and pupil: training to be a wizard can be hard work.

under Yoda's expert tutelage, leaving before he could complete his training in order to attempt to rescue his friends. Already ancient beyond his years, Yoda managed to hang on to life long enough to greet a fully-developed Luke when he returned, before finally dying of old age.

Although he was small, green and wrinkly with droopy ears, spindly limbs and a walking cane, Yoda managed to be a convincing spiritual master. He combined patience with irritability, understanding with insistence, knowledge with power, and although one's abiding impression of him is of a kind being, he was still able to be frightening and awe-inspiring when the need arose. He also had an unusual way of phrasing his sentences, placing the subject at the end of a sentence, rather than its more common location at the beginning – "Strong am I" rather than "I am strong", and "Luminous beings are we", rather than "We are luminous beings".

WORLD: In the old Republic, Yoda was largely based in the capital of Coruscant. An incredible world, Coruscant has been completely built up and built over into one gigantic city that covers the whole globe. Even so, the towers of the city shoot miles up into the sky, and they themselves are overlooked by a maze of floating platforms and suspended walkways and buildings. Coruscant is terminally short of space. The Jedi had a building to serve as their headquarters, but it was destroyed when they were betrayed. The Dagobah system was a significant change. The planet he settled on was a swamp world, heavily populated by wild creatures and other life forms but with no intelligent

✱ Below: Robe, staff and magic powers – Obi-Wan qualifies too.

species. As a planet strong in the darker side of the force – the natural cycle there is vicious and predatory – the planet's natural emanations masked his presence, strong in the light side, from his enemies.

For most of the population of the Empire/Republic, magic is a matter of superstition and mythology. Only those few people who ever come face to face with a Jedi or a Sith ever have the chance of seeing any magic in action. Most people rely on technology to help get through the day. Once the Empire took over and the Jedi were destroyed, knowledge of them was suppressed to discourage their resurgence, and the power of the magic available to them was largely forgotten.

MAGIC: Yoda is a master of the Jedi art, a fascinating blend of wizardry and mysticism. For the Jedi, magic stems from the Force, a flow of universal energy that moves through all things and binds them in a myriad of ways. Using the power of the Force, it is possible to move objects telekinetically, look into the future (and sense the present), control the minds – and bodily functions – of others, enhance yourself, and even manipulate raw energy. The Jedi originally served as the guardians of law and honesty, actively enforcing the rules and regulations of the Republic, and their power in the Force was used to enhance their abilities to serve as super-police. Their foresight made them blindingly fast in combat, because they could see the moves of their opponents before they happened, and physical enhancement added to their strength, speed and agility. In addition, their abilities to control minds and move objects added to their skill at enforcing law.

Spells and rituals play next to no part in Jedi magic. Although the old Jedi art had all the trappings of a religion, with rites of passage and celebration, and

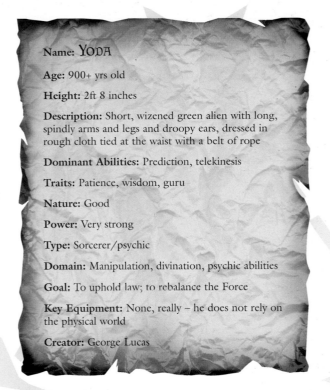

Name: YODA

Age: 900+ yrs old

Height: 2ft 8 inches

Description: Short, wizened green alien with long, spindly arms and legs and droopy ears, dressed in rough cloth tied at the waist with a belt of rope

Dominant Abilities: Prediction, telekinesis

Traits: Patience, wisdom, guru

Nature: Good

Power: Very strong

Type: Sorcerer/psychic

Domain: Manipulation, divination, psychic abilities

Goal: To uphold law; to rebalance the Force

Key Equipment: None, really – he does not rely on the physical world

Creator: George Lucas

formalized language and training, the magic itself is largely concentrated on gestures for channelling the power of the Force. In addition to the sorcerous component, Jedi also possess strong psychic powers, particularly when it comes to sensing physical surroundings and the minds of specific individuals, discerning the way that future events will play out, and feeling the flow of the Force.

The Jedi represent the light side of the Force and are collectively dedicated to law and justice, but their goodness is counterbalanced by the dark side of the Force as embodied in the evil Sith lords. The Sith are the opposites of the Jedi, dedicated to personal gain and power, but they share the same techniques, powers and even many of the quasi-religious rituals and formalities of the Jedi religion. After centuries in hiding, the Sith finally betrayed and destroyed the Jedi, hunting them down and killing them, and used their own powers to take control of the Republic, turning it into the Empire.

Rincewind

The unlikely hero of Terry Pratchett's first two humorous fantasy novels – and of several more further on in the series to boot – Rincewind is the Discworld's most inept wizard. He is a peculiarly fitting hero for the series of hilarious parodies and catalogues of disaster that make up Pratchett's work. Rincewind is one of the Disc's most enduring characters, almost seeming to represent the crazy world itself. With the series running in at more than 20 novels, two computer games, a role-playing game and numerous other items, it looks like he is going to be around a while yet.

BIOGRAPHY: Rincewind was born under the inauspicious constellation known as the "Small Boring Group of Faint Stars", a star-sign traditionally associated with onion-sellers and people who make chessboards. He grew up in the Shades, a particularly dangerous, smelly area of the city of Ankh-Morpork. As the city has a well-deserved reputation for being generally dangerous and smelly itself, the Shades is the sort of area that tourists stumble into by mistake, only to emerge several days later as dog-food. The River Ankh, which divides the metropolis into the old cities of Ankh and Morpork, is so full of sewage, pollution, mud and other rubbish that it is generally thought to slither rather than flow.

Despite this unlikely start to his wizarding career, Rincewind managed to get into the Unseen University, the greatest academy of the magical arts on the Discworld. Once there, his lack of any real magical talent was totally overshadowed when, on a dare, he opened a magical grimoire called the Octavo that held the eight Great Spells used by the creator to make the world. One of the spells escaped into Rincewind's head, and stayed there. Other spells didn't dare share his mind with a spell of that ferociousness. The finest wizards of the Faculty of Medicine were unable to remove it, leaving Rincewind magically castrated. Worst of all, whenever he was run-down, the spell would try to force him to speak, and no one knew whether or not that would unmake the world.

After graduation, Rincewind was still unable to perform magic, and scratched out a living as a petty translator until he met Twoflower, the Discworld's

first tourist. After initially trying to con Twoflower out of enough gold to set him up for life, Rincewind was persuaded, at sword-point, to act as a guide for the tourist. They stumbled through a number of cataclysmic adventures, including being attacked by an evil elder god, kidnapped by riders of imaginary dragons, and falling off the edge of the world in a golden fish, until Rincewind finally managed to banish the spell from his mind and Twoflower went home.

Even after getting rid of the great spell, Rincewind proved a failure as a wizard. Still unable to master even the most basic magic, he spent a period of time acting as an assistant to the university librarian, who had been magically transformed into an orang-utan some time before. After a brief period stuck in the dungeon dimensions, he was accidentally summoned back onto the Disc again by a careless demonologist called Eric. Other adventures naturally followed. Rincewind was last seen making his way in the lost continent of "Forecks", still cheerfully unable to muster any magical forces.

WORLD: The Discworld is magical in much the same way that the universe is really rather big. It is a physically impossible realm, brought into existence because an infinitely varied universe demands it somewhere. The Discworld itself is, as the name suggests, a flat, circular planet. It rests on the back of four great elephants, named Berilia, Tubul, Jerakeen and Great T'Phon. These mighty creatures in turn stand upon the back of Great A'Tuin, a gigantic star turtle swimming endlessly through the seas of space. A small sun,

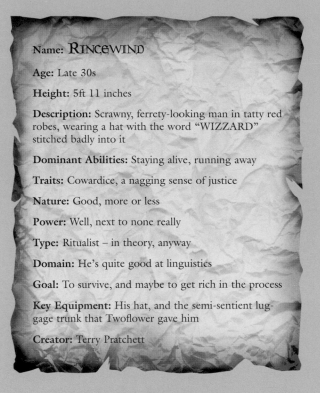

Name: RINCEWIND

Age: Late 30s

Height: 5ft 11 inches

Description: Scrawny, ferrety-looking man in tatty red robes, wearing a hat with the word "WIZZARD" stitched badly into it

Dominant Abilities: Staying alive, running away

Traits: Cowardice, a nagging sense of justice

Nature: Good, more or less

Power: Well, next to none really

Type: Ritualist – in theory, anyway

Domain: He's quite good at linguistics

Goal: To survive, and maybe to get rich in the process

Key Equipment: His hat, and the semi-sentient luggage trunk that Twoflower gave him

Creator: Terry Pratchett

➤ Below: The Discworld is so magical that wizardry is hardly worth the effort.

swords and special potions through to werewolves, gnomes and even sentient trees. The Disc's inhabitants don't believe in magic, in the same way that we don't believe in traffic – it's not a matter of belief, because it's all around you. It simply exists, and belief doesn't come into it. Discworld wizards tend to be a fairly complacent lot, more interested in their academic tenures and sorting out their next meal than in probing the secrets of the universe.

Unseen University, in Ankh-Morpork, is the most important seat of magical learning on the Disc. Its main building is a large, sprawling, gothic-style affair with all sorts of wings, towers, basements and annexes. The internal layout is somewhat unpredictable, and all sorts of surprises lie in wait for the unwary, particularly in the vicinity of the magical, high-energy research laboratories. The Great Hall, where meals are served, remains predictably stable.

no more than a mile across, endlessly circles the disc, providing day and night to its inhabitants. On a planet like that, pretty much anything can happen.

Magic on the Discworld is so common as to be almost routine. Any number of petty soothsayers, hedge-doctors, witches, alchemists and priests can be found. All sorts of things are magical, from talking

MAGIC: Discworld magic is really rather hard work, and not usually considered worth all the effort. It can take months or years to memorize a spell prior to casting it, and once it's ready, the ritual involved may take hours of work, and require all sorts of unusual ingredients. Frankly, it's all just too much bother. Therefore, most wizards concern themselves with far more sensible pursuits than spell casting – lunch, for example. Rincewind, having had a great many adventures, is considered, well, a bit *peculiar* by the other wizards.

The Wizard of Oz

L. Frank Baum created one of the most enduring fairytales of the modern world with his prodigious series of books based in the land of Oz. Its most famous portrayal was in the 1939 film *The Wizard of Oz*. This was based primarily on Baum's book *The Wonderful Wizard of Oz*, published in 1900. In it, a young Kansas orphan called Dorothy and her dog Toto are transported – perhaps dreaming – into the magical fairytale kingdom of Oz. The mysterious Wizard who gives his name to the film rules this kingdom. *The Wonderful Wizard of Oz* was the first book Baum published about the kingdom, and he wrote 13 more books about the land between 1904 and his death in 1919, eight more than he had originally planned. Other writers took up where he left off, and there are now 40 works that are considered canonical (i.e. genuinely accurate) stories about the land. Despite being seen by many people as the definitive Oz story, the 1939 *The Wizard of Oz* film itself is just one of 17 different films based on Baum's works. It is the most respected of them all by far, however.

Biography: Oscar Zoroaster Phadrig Isaac Norman Henkle Emanuel Ambroise Diggs was born in Omaha, Nebraska in 1828, the son of a local politician. Almost from the first, the child felt weighed

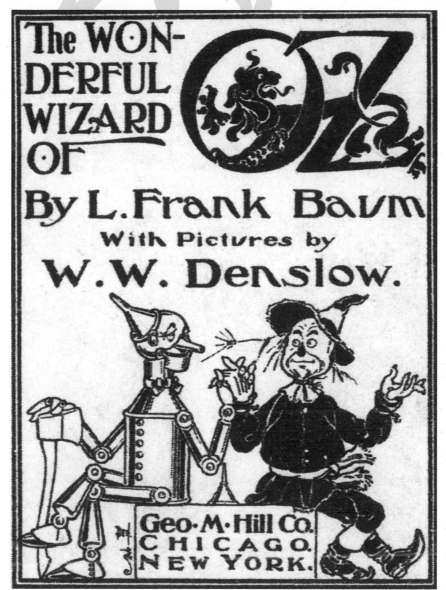

THE WON-
DERFUL
WIZARD
OF Oz
By L. Frank Baum
With Pictures by
W.W. Denslow.

Geo. M. Hill Co.
CHICAGO.
NEW YORK.

★ Left: The original book cover.

down by the burden of such a long and cumbersome name. Aware that his initials spelt out "ozpinhead", Oscar grew up calling himself O.Z., dropping the "P.I.N.H.E.A.D." part as an unreasonable slur on his intelligence. Perhaps because of resentment about his name, Oscar ran away from home while still a young man, and joined a circus. He learnt to do tricks – ventriloquism, stage magic and hot-air ballooning – and became a skilled sideshow performer. To make sure the audience got the right idea, he called himself

✷ Top: The Wizard and Dorothy (as played by
Judy Garland) prepare to set off.

✷ Right: Life can be a witch sometimes. The Wicked Witch
of the West and one of her fabulous flying monkeys.

a wizard, and stencilled his initials on his balloon and on other pieces of equipment.

One afternoon, a wind blew him and his balloon away from the circus and out over the desert. After a time, he arrived over the four countries of the Munchkins, the Gillikins, the Winkies and the Quadlings, each one ruled over by a witch. Oscar declared himself a wizard, and everyone deferred to him, already being impressed with his arrival from the air. He ordered the locals to build the emerald city at the point where the four countries touched each other, and declared himself the ruler of the land of Oz. He ruled Oz in peace for many years, eventually becoming old and homesick. When Dorothy arrived, blown in by a cyclone, he agreed to carry her back home again. The balloon proved beyond his control again, and he was blown off. Dorothy got home anyway, and Oscar eventually got back to Omaha.

Once there, he discovered that all his old friends had died or moved away, and he returned to Oz again. The land was now ruled by the rightful Princess, Ozma, and Oscar was made her official Wizard. Under tuition from the Good Witch Glinda, he eventually went on to gain a diploma from the Eastern Evian University of Magic, and become a genuine, bona fide spell-caster rather than a humbug wizard.

WORLD: The land of Oz is one of the faerie realms, and as such magic is a common and everyday part of life. All sorts of magical creatures and people can be found, so much so that people are divided roughly into "meat" and "non-meat" – people made of flesh and blood and bone, like Dorothy and Glinda, and people made of other things, such as the Tin Man and the Scarecrow. In addition to the evil witches of the West and East that Dorothy "liqui-dates", there are two evil witches, Mombi and Singra, who had ruled the North and South until the good witches Glinda and Locasta defeat and exile them. The evil Mombi goes on to cause much trouble throughout the series of books, as does Roquat the evil Nome King.

MAGIC: Wizardly magic in Oz conforms to stereotype fantasy patterns – there is a higgledy-piggledy mixture of spells, rituals, gestures and magical objects. A chant can make the Wizard pass through a closed door without opening it, but a spell is required to make him invisible, and herbs sprinkled on his head turn him temporarily to wood. In general, Oz magic is powerful but not cataclysmic. What it lacks in sheer firepower, however, it makes up for by being a major part of daily life.

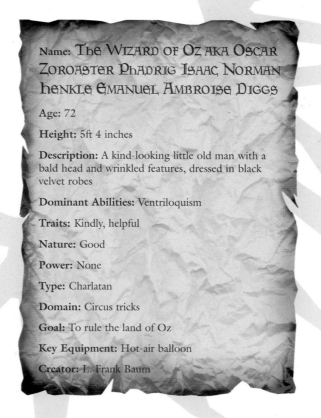

Name: THE WIZARD OF OZ AKA OSCAR ZOROASTER PHADRIG ISAAC NORMAN HENKLE EMANUEL AMBROISE DIGGS

Age: 72

Height: 5ft 4 inches

Description: A kind-looking little old man with a bald head and wrinkled features, dressed in black velvet robes

Dominant Abilities: Ventriloquism

Traits: Kindly, helpful

Nature: Good

Power: None

Type: Charlatan

Domain: Circus tricks

Goal: To rule the land of Oz

Key Equipment: Hot-air balloon

Creator: L. Frank Baum

Abdul al-Hazred

The cycle of stories known as the Cthulhu Mythos were created by Howard Phillips Lovecraft, an American horror writer born in 1890. In these stories, he set out his terrifying view of the world as a tiny spot of pleasant light in a universe of dark evil. Humanity, according to Lovecraft, teeters on the edge of a gigantic abyss, which could reach up to engulf the Earth at any time. Everything we believe in is apparently false; the true lords and masters of Earth are supposed to be a collection of foul, monstrous Elder Gods, locked away from our reality for a short time, but ready to return "when the stars are right". Cthulhu itself is one of these vile deities. Lovecraft's work is still stark and disturbing, and it has been a major influence on our literature and film – not just in

★ Right: Howard Phillips Lovecraft.

horror, but in other areas as well. Throughout the stories of the Cthulhu Mythos, the one corrupting influence that crops up time and again is the *Necronomicon*. This evil tome of magic details Cthulhu and its fellows, and provides spells by which the servants of the Elder Gods can be called forth and compelled to do foul deeds. To read the *Necronomicon* is to be driven mad … but the *Necronomicon* itself is a translation of an earlier manuscript, the *Kitab al-Azif*, written by the mad Arab, Abdul al-Hazred.

BIOGRAPHY: Abdul al-Hazred (or more correctly *Abd al-Azir*, "Worshipper of the Great Devourer") lived in the late seventh/early eighth centuries AD. Born in Sanaa in Yemen, he was a poet and philosopher who found a degree of artistic success and acceptance during the period of the Ommiade caliphs, some time around 700AD. Something of a student of magic, astronomy and early science, he toured around ancient Arabia looking for inspiration and secrets, and was accounted mad. He journeyed through the ruins of Babylon, and in the labyrinths beneath the Egyptian temple city of Memphis, before going out alone into the great southern desert – the *Roba al Khaliyeh* or "Empty Space" of the ancient Arabs, known more recently as the *Dahma* or "Crimson" desert. Many strange tales and marvels are told by the few who have penetrated into the desert and returned alive, stories of the jealously protective evil spirits who live there, and the lethal monsters that keep them company. Al-Hazred spent his time in the *Roba al Khaliyeh* listening to the spirits and the monsters, and exploring the region. He claimed to have visited the long-lost, evil city of pillars, Irem, buried beneath the shifting sands, and learned strange things in a hidden room. It was a nameless desert town that proved to be

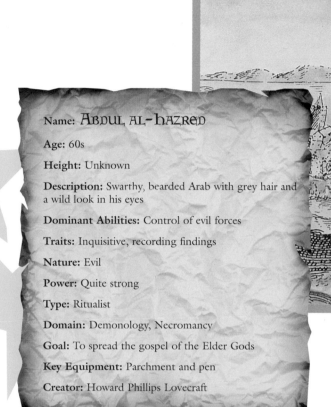

Name: ABDUL AL-HAZRED

Age: 60s

Height: Unknown

Description: Swarthy, bearded Arab with grey hair and a wild look in his eyes

Dominant Abilities: Control of evil forces

Traits: Inquisitive, recording findings

Nature: Evil

Power: Quite strong

Type: Ritualist

Domain: Demonology, Necromancy

Goal: To spread the gospel of the Elder Gods

Key Equipment: Parchment and pen

Creator: Howard Phillips Lovecraft

his greatest find, however. Beneath the ruins, he found documents detailing the horrifying secrets and legends of a race of gods far older than mankind. This work provided much of the information that went into the *Kitab al-Azif*. On his return from the *Roba*, he settled in Damascus, where he wrote the *al-Azif*. Shortly after its completion, according to his twelfth century biographer, Ebn Khallikan, he was seized by one or more invisible monsters in broad daylight in the middle of a bustling bazaar, and ripped to shreds as horrified witnesses looked on.

WORLD: The title of the *Kitab al-Azif* translates approximately into English as "the screeching of the desert demons", although Lovecraft normally rendered it more poetically. The fictional book may have actually been loosely inspired by the work *Kutu Kitab Katulu*, housed in the British Library. The mythology that the *al-Azif* portrays holds that the Elder Gods are locked away, but it does make some rather shocking allegations about a race of aliens who created humanity and the other animals. These creatures lived in gigantic cities now locked under the Antarctic ice sheet. Other occasional monsters apparently lurk in the hidden places of the earth as well, in lonely forests and quiet mountainsides, generally keeping out of the way of humanity. In general, though, true magic is very rare and more or less unknown.

MAGIC: Abdul al-Hazred's magic is dedicated mainly to the summoning, control and manipulation of the Elder Gods and their servants. The spells he lists in the *Kitab al-Azif* seem to be flawed, however, either through his madness or in their translation, as most attempts to work with the techniques in the *Necronomicon* seem to end in disaster. Some wizards, however, have been able to correct or fine-tune the formulae involved not only to summon and control monsters, but also to raise the dead and switch bodies with other people, gain eternal youth, and uncover all sorts of long-forgotten secrets. The most famous excerpt from the *Necronomicon* however is not a spell, but a warning of what Lovecraft alleged was still to come – "That is not dead which can eternal lie, and with strange aeons even death may die."

✦ Right: Lovecraft sitting among his most famous creations.

YoG-SOTHOTH
Knows the gate
YoG-SOTH gate

That is not d
which can eternal
And with strang
even death may

H.P. Lovecraft
1890 ≈ 1937

The Sorcerer's Apprentice

The story of the Sorcerer's Apprentice is genuinely ancient. Although the character is most famous now for the eight-minute feature segment in Walt Disney's animated classic *Fantasia*, it has a long history. The Disney section, originally from 1940, is animated to accompany an orchestral scherzo of the same name by Paul Dukas, premiered in Paris in 1897. Dukas based his piece on *Der Zauberlehrling*, a ballad-like poem written in 1796 by the German writer, Johann Wolfgang von Goethe. This poem was in turn based on *The Lie-Fancier*, a tale recorded by the ancient Greek satirist, Lucian of Samosata, in 150AD. Lucian himself is thought to have been rewriting a story that came out of ancient pharonic Egypt, and may have even pre-dated it. As such, the tale of the Sorcerer's Apprentice has an ancient pedigree, and has remained largely unchanged as it has passed down the centuries.

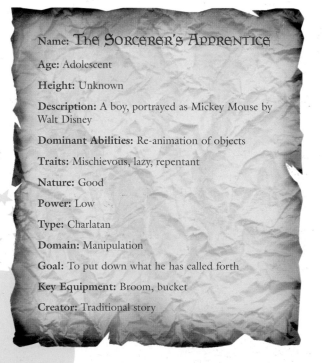

✦ Above: Things are going well for the Sorcerer's Apprentice: scene from *Fantasia*.

✦ Above: Mickey, as the Apprentice, makes his first mistake.

BIOGRAPHY: The original story of the Sorcerer's Apprentice is almost as simple as the version retold in *Fantasia*. A village boy goes to the castle of a local sorcerer and asks for his help in getting some food for the village. In return, the sorcerer takes the boy on as his apprentice and starts teaching him magic. Tiring of his chores one afternoon, the boy takes advantage of the sorcerer's absence to use a spell he has seen his master use. He uses the magic to animate a broom, so that it will fetch pails of water for him from the well. All works as planned, until the apprentice realizes that he doesn't know how to stop the broom. The castle quickly starts to fill with water. In desperation, the boy chops the broom in two, but finds that both parts

Name: THE SORCERER'S APPRENTICE

Age: Adolescent

Height: Unknown

Description: A boy, portrayed as Mickey Mouse by Walt Disney

Dominant Abilities: Re-animation of objects

Traits: Mischievous, lazy, repentant

Nature: Good

Power: Low

Type: Charlatan

Domain: Manipulation

Goal: To put down what he has called forth

Key Equipment: Broom, bucket

Creator: Traditional story

✦ Above: An early
portrayal of the
Sorcerer's Apprentice.

continue the work, filling the castle twice as quickly as before. Finally, just before the situation becomes totally disastrous, the sorcerer returns, banishes the magic, and sets everything right. Chastened, the boy returns to his studies and duties properly, and in due time learns all his master's magic. At that point, the sorcerer turns himself into a toad and leaves the area, handing the castle over to the new sorcerer, who can give as much food to the village as is necessary.

WORLD: *The Sorcerer's Apprentice* is a fable, set within a fairytale-like land. As such, the sorcerer and his magic are part of reality, but stand outside everyday events, representing a special solution to the problem of hunger. Within the framework of the tale, magic is a plot device used to represent the limitations of knowledge. It is never really explored or explained; it

is just there to make the story work and to help it carry its point effectively. The real message of *The Sorcerer's Apprentice*, of course, is that a little knowledge can be dangerous – don't assume that just because you can do something, that you should do it, or that you can undo it once you have started.

MAGIC: The magic used to animate, and later quieten, the broom is assumed within the framework of the story to be a fairly simple spell, with limited gestures and no real ritual of any significance. The Apprentice knows more magic than just how to start the broom, but either the crisis forces his knowledge out of his mind, or it is of no real significance to the situation he finds himself in, because he does not attempt to fall back on it, and we never learn what it might be.

honourable Mentions

There are a great many wizards of all shapes and sizes who are worthy of further consideration, but sadly we don't have the room to go into them in the proper detail. They include mad, cackling **Tim the Enchanter** from *Monty Python and the Holy Grail*, who casts fireballs around convulsively and teleports himself from place to place; **Belgarath, Garion** and the brotherhood of immortal sorcerers from *The Belgariad* books by David Eddings; **Will Stanton** and **Merriman Lyon**, youngest and oldest members of the Circle of Old Ones who work for the Light in its endless struggle to stop the Dark from taking over the earth in the *Dark is Rising* sequence by Susan Cooper; super-powerful wizards **Pug** and **Macros** from Raymond Feist's *Riftwar* Saga; **Rand al-Thor** and the other **Aes Sedai** destined to break the world in Robert Jordan's *Wheel of Time* series; and diverse other worthies such as **Ningauble of the Seven Eyes** & **Sheelba of the Eyeless Face, Shimrod** scion of **Murgen, Rhialto the Marvellous; Raistlin; Arithon Prince of Shadow; Sir Adam Sinclair** and many more.

✦ Below: John Cleese as Tim the Enchanter.

47 ········· Magical Characters

The myths and legends of the past play an important part in our world. All through history, humans have used thrilling stories of mighty heroes, villains and gods to make sense of the world, the universe, moral issues, and even birth, sex and death. A society's myths bind it together, helping to give it definition and character.

Important Legendary Wizards from Around the World

Because of this, although the modern world has moved away from traditional forms of storytelling, the myths and legends of the world continue to provide both inspiration and background. We now have television, cinema, CDs and computer games to tell us stories, but the people who actually produce our entertainment continue to draw imagery and tales from our myths, wrapping them up in modern forms. *Buffy the Vampire Slayer* would have been perfectly at home at an ancient Greek campfire, next to stories about Hercules or Odysseus.

Wizards are a vital part of myths and legends all around the world. Heroes are exceptional, by definition – that means that they need exceptional powers, and exceptional enemies. Sometimes the hero him- or herself is a wizard, calling on magic tricks to win the day, while other times a friendly wizard acts as advisor, providing enough help to make the task possible, but never enough to make it easy. Sometimes, it is the villain who is a wizard, using magic to cause all sorts of problems. Often, the wizards in legends remain nameless plot devices to make the hero look good, being just "a wizard". Some mythic wizards are much more than that, though. Their very names have power, and shout down to us through the centuries, carrying the old tales with them. The greatest wizard of all, the most famous, the most flawed, was Merlin.

✴ Left: Merlin amd Arthur claim Excalibur.

✴ Below: Buffy, as played by Sarah Michelle Gellar, is a true mythic hero.

Merlin

The myths and legends of King Arthur and the Knights of the Round Table form a vivid, colourful cycle of wonders and betrayals. The stories, set in the golden age of Arthur's rule of Britain, are a fascinating tapestry across time. Some come from the earliest Celtic accounts of Camelot some 1,500 years ago, while other elements were added when Britain became a Christian country. It was further expanded by French and German stories in early medieval times, and tied together into a great romance, *Le Morte D' Arthur*, by the fifteenth-century poet Thomas Malory. Merlin is a central figure of the myths, Arthur's wizardly advisor who helped him to conceive and form Camelot itself.

BIOGRAPHY: The most famous mythological wizard, Merlin (originally Myrrdin) was born after his mother, a Christian nun, was raped by a demon. At the moment of his birth, fearing that the child might take after its evil father, his mother snatched him up and plunged him into a fount of holy water. Although this wise treatment gave him a deep-seated love of the mortal world and the desire to help humanity out as much as possible, he also kept some of his father's qualities. This included the ability to change shape, a powerful driving restlessness that made him a wanderer, a mastery of the magical arts, and an extremely strong sexual appetite.

He was raised by the witch Nimue (sometimes Niniane or Viviane), a fellow shape-changer who fell in love with him as he became an adult. Merlin rejected her, however, and went out into the mortal world. The adult Merlin spent much of his time appearing as a wise old man. In this guise, he acted as a wizardly adviser to a number of early kings and warlords, including High King Vortigern and Uther Pendragon.

✦ Far Right: Merlin imprisioned by Nimue ...

✦ Below: ... and with her before his betrayal.

✦ Right: A decorative seal depicting the wizard at rest.

Whilst still a child, Merlin was found by soldiers working for Vortigern. The King was busily trying to build a fort on a rocky hillside in Wales, and the structure kept collapsing. Merlin was imprisoned underground and threatened with sacrifice if he did not tell the King what was going wrong. He dutifully explained to Vortigern where he was going wrong – the rock actually had objections to the castle, which needed to be overcome – and went on to prophesy his downfall, which indeed came to be. Next, working as the advisor of Ambrosius Aurelianus, Merlin was responsible for the creation of Stonehenge, erected in celebration of Amrosius' reign.

Uther Pendragon later demanded supernatural help from Merlin to become supreme ruler of Britain. Merlin refused, telling him that his ambitions would fail and that he would destroy his own line. Uther took no notice, and demanded the power to change shape. Merlin agreed, transforming Uther into the likeness of a rival, King Gorlois of Tintagel, the ruler of Cornwall. Uther was infatuated with Gorlois'

queen, Ygern, and once he looked like her husband, he immediately went to have sex with her.

Ygern became pregnant, and her son, the young Arthur, was raised in secret by Merlin. Partly as a result of Merlin's teachings, Arthur was able to pull Uther's sword from the stone his father had embedded it in, and unite Britain as King, fighting against the Romans. When the sword broke in a duel with a giant, Merlin guided Arthur to the Lady of the Lake. A hand rose out of the water holding the magical sword Excalibur, whose edge never blunted and whose scabbard stopped

★ Right: Arthur is
presented with his birthright.

★ Far Right: "Oh yesss, yess,
good." Nicol Williamson's
superb portrayal of
Merlin in *Excalibur*.

bleeding. Arthur was given the sword for the duration of his reign.

At other times, however, Merlin's demonic nature would exert a hold. Sometimes he would transform himself into an extremely handsome young man, and wander around the country seducing every girl he came across. At other times, he would disappear entirely from the mortal world. He particularly enjoyed spending time as a stream of water, a breeze, a cloud in the sky, or even just a thought, whispering through the world.

It was his lustful nature that eventually proved his downfall. Nimue, devastated by Merlin's rejection, decided to seek revenge on him. She changed herself into every shape she could imagine to trap him, and each time he was wary enough, and smart enough, to escape from her. Finally, she turned herself into a

beautiful woman, and allowed him to seduce her. Merlin's lust blinded him to her true identity, and he made love to her. At the moment of ecstasy, when all his defences were down and he was fully distracted, she changed herself into a sphere of amber and engulfed him completely. Once he was trapped, she transformed into an oak tree. They remain locked together still.

WORLD: Merlin is primarily remembered for his place in the Arthurian myths. They are set in the middle of the first millennium AD, when the Romans occupying Britain were losing their grip on even their safest territories, and the country was reverting to a collection of petty territories ruled by warlord kings. Arthur united the country, defeating the Romans and various Viking chieftains, and bringing all the territories under his rule. He ushered in a time of justice, law and fairness for all the land, and ruled wisely from Camelot during a golden period. His wife Guinevere, who had an affair with Lancelot, his finest knight, later betrayed Arthur and the innocence of his reign was shattered. The quest for the Holy Grail followed, and finally the war with Morgan, Arthur's half-sister, and their son Mordred, which saw the end of the period, and Arthur taken away by the faeries of Avalon to sleep until the world needed him again. This was a period rich in supernatural occurrences; faeries, witches, shape-shifters and monsters were common in the land. The rituals of superstition guarded the common people against magic threats lurking in wait. Merlin, being only half-human, stood between the worlds of normality and of faerie, and acted as a protector of the people.

MAGIC: The styles and patterns of Merlin's magic have varied through the years with each different storyteller, so it is difficult to be certain exactly what

process he followed. Some accounts have Merlin speaking spells, while others indicate that his magic came from his mind alone. The most famous incarnation of Merlin in modern times was Nicol Williamson's frightening portrayal of the role in the classic 1981 movie *Excalibur*. This showed him as a strong, aloof man in a metal skullcap, almost alien in outlook and interests, sharing little in common with the mortals around him – his magic was accomplished with the aid of one versatile spell, the "Charm of Making". Whichever format is taken for Merlin's powers, he is consistently able to see into the future, change his form, talk with spirits and control the elements around him.

Name: MERLIN

Age: Immortal

Height: Varies

Description: As a wizard, he appears as an elderly man with long white hair and beard, carrying a staff

Dominant Abilities: Divination, transformation

Traits: Helpful, sympathetic, restless, driven, lustful

Nature: Good

Power: Very strong

Type: Sorcerer, mostly

Domain: Elementalist, particularly with respect to nature

Goal: To help humanity

Key Equipment: None in particular, but he did personally make the Round Table, cause Stonehenge to be built, and lead Arthur to Excalibur.

Taliesin the Bard

The tradition of sorcerer-bards is strong in Welsh folklore. Taliesin was the greatest of all the bards, blessed with all the knowledge in the world and a radiant, shining beauty. It is generally believed that the legendary stories surrounding Taliesin were created to flatter and honour a real man of the same name, who was court bard to the Welsh kings in the sixth century AD, and who is believed to be buried at a village that was named after him.

BIOGRAPHY: Caridwen was a witch, and with her husband, Tegid Voel, she lived in the middle of Lake Tegid in Penllyn, and they had three children. Their eldest child, Morvan ab Tegid, was a normal son. Their second child was a daughter, Creirwy, the most beautiful maiden in the entire world. Their third child, however, a son named Avagddu, was as ugly as his sister was lovely. Caridwen despaired for Avagddu, thinking that because he was so ill favoured he would never win acceptance in the world, and so decided to give him the gift of knowledge and wisdom. She set out to brew a potion that would contain all of the knowledge, inspiration and magic in the world, which she could then feed to her son. To create the potion she desired, the cauldron had to be stirred, boiling, without end for a year and a day, until finally three drops would be yielded that would contain all the world's wisdom.

Gwion Bach was the son of Gwreang of Llanfair, born in Caereinion in Powys. Gwion was captured by the witch Caridwen, and put to work stirring her cauldron. She also caught a blind man named Morda, and set him to feeding the fire beneath it. She threatened them with dire fates if the cauldron should stop boiling. While they toiled, she studied books written by ancient astronomers and, during the correct planetary times and alignments, went out to collect all sorts of charm-carrying herbs to add to her brew.

The cauldron continued to brew until one day, towards the end of the year, Gwion was slightly careless in his stirring. While Caridwen was off gathering herbs and speaking spells to prepare them, three drops of the enchanted brew splashed out of the cauldron and struck Gwion on the finger. Because they were so hot, having been boiled for nearly a year, he sucked his painful finger. As soon as the drops went into his mouth, he gained the power of the brew, and suddenly foresaw everything that was to come. Realizing that the witch meant to kill him and Morda after the year was up, and

........Chapter Three

★ Right: Caridwen with her cauldron.

★ Far Right: Taliesin plays to inspire the harts.

a piece of wood and hit Morda so hard around the head with it that one of his eyes fell out. He protested that she was being unfair by wounding him, because he was not to blame. Then Caridwen saw the truth of it – Gwion had benefited from her work, and so she went after him.

At first she ran after the boy, but when he saw her, he turned himself into a hare and sped off. She responded by turning into a greyhound, and chased him down. Before she could grab him though, he dashed to a river and turned into a fish. She transformed into an otter to pursue him, and he had to turn into a bird and fly away to escape her jaws. Even so, she became a hawk and shot after him, harrying him. Finally, terrified for his life, Gwion saw a heap of wheat on a bare floor, and dropped amongst it, turning himself into another grain of wheat. Caridwen saw him, however, and changed herself into a high-crested black hen. She scratched amongst the wheat until she found the grain that was Gwion, and ate him.

That was not the end, however. Having consumed the Gwion grain, she carried him with her for nine months, and finally gave birth to a child of radiant beauty, Taliesin. He was so beautiful that she couldn't bring herself to kill him after all, and instead she wrapped him in a leather sack and cast him out to

perceiving suddenly the great power and skill of Caridwen, Gwion fled off back towards his old home in Powys. The cauldron, meanwhile, split into two halves, because its contents were now poisonous without the three drops.

When Caridwen returned with the day's herbs, she found the cauldron broken, her hopes dashed and her year's work wasted, and she was furious. She grabbed float off to sea on 29 April, where the gods could decide what to do with him.

As luck would have it, he floated into the salmon weir of King Gwyddno Garanhir, which the king emptied every May eve. The king's son, Elphin, known throughout the kingdom for being unlucky, was emptying the weir that year. To Elphin's horror, the weir, which normally held a hundred pounds worth of fish, held only the leather sack. However, his luck was shown to have turned when he opened the sack and set Taliesin free. The child consoled him with a prophetic poem, foretelling fortune and honour for Elphin, and saying that he himself would be of more worth to the king's son than 300 salmon.

As he matured, Taliesin went on to become the greatest poet and bard that Wales would ever see. He had the gifts of prophecy and knowledge, understood science, and could use his songs and music to work all sorts of wonders. He could calm storms with a word, incite people to peace, love, bravery or frenzy, control the weather, bring fertility to plants and animals, open locks, travel through time and space and make himself invisible. The tales of his exploits include visiting a number of biblical figures – God in heaven, Noah in the ark, Jonah in the whale and Satan in his kitchen – as well as watching Romulus and Remus build the walls of ancient Rome, and guiding King Arthur into the underworld of Annwn to steal the Cauldron of Plenty, which could provide prosperity and immortality.

WORLD: The myths and legends of the Celtic peoples were greatly eroded by Christian influence. The Christians saw the Celtic myths as vile devil-worship, and did their best to convert the tales and legends into a framework that they felt better about. This combined with the Roman persecution of the Celts across Europe, means the myths that remain are mostly fragmented remnants of what would have once been a rich and powerful tradition. The underworld, Annwn, was a major feature of most stories. All the faeries, demons and goblins lived in this invisible realm, taking on characteristics and identities when they encroached onto the living world. For the people of the time, all sorts of threats apparently lurked just on the edges of normal life, and the rituals of superstition were all that kept the mischievous and malicious spirits away. Taliesin, with his magic and his songs, may have represented the power of knowledge.

MAGIC: Most of Taliesin's power lay within his music. It was through his songs or his playing that he was able to work most of the wonders that he did, and his prophecies, too, were always couched in verse, and usually sung. Against the usual run of this trend, his ability to change shape was spontaneous, requiring no active spell casting.

Name: TALIESIN

Age: Varies

Height: 6ft

Description: An extremely handsome young man with a radiant brow

Dominant Abilities: Evocation, divination, transformation

Traits: Creative, musical, just

Nature: Good

Power: Strong

Type: Magic channels mostly through song

Domain: General

Goal: To create works of beauty and help the weak

Key Equipment: His harp

The Yellow Emperor

The traditional creator of China's Daoist religion, the Yellow Emperor; is still respected and honoured as one of the great civilizing forces of the country. The forces of heaven and hell play a large part in traditional Chinese mythology, where every being, mortal or immortal, has a specific role to fulfil.

BIOGRAPhY: The Yellow Emperor, Huang Di, ruled China 5,000 years ago. He was the first of the mythic Five Emperors, a dynasty of wise sorcerer-rulers who steered China from barbarism and chaos into civilized order. Like his later brethren, the Yellow Emperor had the power to change his shape and appearance, and lived slightly outside time, so that he aged far more slowly than most mortals.

Even from the moment of his birth, the Yellow Emperor was knowledgeable and wise. He was born knowing mighty magic and was able to speak all of the languages of the world, as well as knowing everything that the people of Earth at that time knew. He devoted himself to bringing knowledge and enlightenment, and taught the people of China how to hunt, fish, farm and build roads. He then went on to invent a great number of different innovations based on the knowledge that he held, including the wheel, armour, weaponry, ships, the compass, coins, law and government. During his small amounts of spare time, he entertained himself by creating music, pottery, painting, poetry and other arts. His wife, meanwhile, discovered how to make silk, and his chief official created writing.

On top of everything else, the Yellow Emperor was in frequent communication with the gods in heaven. He was permitted to climb the holy mountain, Tai Shan, in order to speak with them through prayers

✦ Left: The Yellow Emperor, mythic creator of Daoism.

and sacrifices. He travelled up the mountain in an ivory chariot. This vehicle's driver was a green crane with a human face, and six dragons and an elephant pulled it. The chariot was followed by processions of phoenixes, snakes, tigers and wolves. When he reached the top of the mountain, the Yellow Empcror would take his place at the centre, and alter his shape until he had four faces, so that he could gaze out at the four quarters of the earth.

The Yellow Emperor's golden reign was calm and prosperous – apart from one short period when the rain god and the wind god rebelled against him – and he himself spent the years presiding over continual feasts and merry-making. For 15 generations, he ruled China wisely. Eventually, however, the endless feasts took their toll, and he started to become fat and slow. He immediately abandoned his luxury, and went to

live in a grass-roofed hut in the palace grounds, fasting and praying.

Eventually, he had a dream of a calm paradise where the inhabitants felt no pain, sorrow or longing, foreswore emotion, and lived revelling in the pure bliss of the spiritual state. When he woke up, he announced that he had discovered Dao, "the way."

His reign lasted for just one more generation, during which time he set forth the eight-fold tenets of Daoism, and invented healing, including Qi Gong and acupuncture. Finally, his work complete, the Yellow Emperor was honoured by being taken up to heaven, and his followers mourned him for 200 years.

WORLD: Back at its early beginnings, the Chinese

empire was a broad mix of peasant smallholdings, nomadic tribes and occasional bandit fiefdoms, with very little in the way of internal structure. Technology was almost non-existent, and the world was seen to be populated by all manner of gods and spirits. The Yellow Emperor brought technological advancement and consistent internal government to the Empire. In the minds of the people, that was far greater magic than any of his sorcerous tricks. He remains one of the greatest cultural heroes of Daoism.

MAGIC: Much of the Yellow Emperor's power came from the rightful authority that he held as the mandated lord of the people on Earth. As such, quite a lot of his magic boiled down to having the right to order spirits and godlings around. On other occasions, he made use of the kind of convoluted ritual traditional to Chinese folklore, involving spells, complex gestures, written formulae on parchment, burning herbs, bells and gongs, and other similar items.

Circe

Gods and goddesses were a familiar part of the daily routine for the ancient Greeks. They meddled continually in mortal affairs, passed on omens and warnings, pulled tricks on people, slept with them, sent them on quests, and generally manipulated them left, right and centre. Half-god heroes and villains, both humans and monsters, were to be found all over the countryside. In many ways, the divine world was there for everyone in much the same way that the adult world is there for young children – all around, but, somehow, you don't quite get to take part in it properly. This familiarity between gods and humans made them extremely intimate, which is perhaps why even now, 2,000 years later, they are still a vibrant part of our culture – as shows like *Hercules: The Legendary Journeys* and *Xena: Warrior Princess* attest.

BIOGRAPHY: One of the most notorious sorceresses of Greek legend, Circe was the daughter of a liaison between the Sun and Hecate, the goddess of black magic, who took the form of an ocean nymph to seduce him. Circe inherited stunning beauty and grace from her father, and great magical prowess – and a rather nasty streak – from her mother. Her double nature caused her continual problems, making her desire a normal life, but also forcing her to angry displays of magical power over petty issues. Like many children of a god, she had a huge appetite for sexual intercourse with mortals.

Circle fell in love with and courted an Italian prince named Picus, but he turned her down. When she realized that she would not be able to have him, she transformed him into a woodpecker. She next turned her affections to a minor sea god called Glaucus, but discovered that he preferred her half-sister, the lovely sea sprite, Scylla. Furious, Circe transformed Scylla into a hideous sea-monster; human from the waist up but below the waist she was left with 12 dog's legs and six snarling, fang-toothed heads on long, snaky necks. Circe actually went so far as to

marry the prince of the state of Colchis, but found the idea of giving up her powers to live in his harem too objectionable. She killed him instead, in an attempt to seize his throne. Her father, the Sun, rescued her from the furious subjects of Colchis, and gave her the float-ing island of Aeaea to rule in an attempt to keep her out of trouble.

Circe spent her time on Aeaea sitting at a loom in her palace singing a song – a song so beautiful that none could resist it. When sailors landed on the island,

Right: Circe sits in her beautiful gardens.

her song would bring them to the palace. Once a "guest" arrived, she would treat him to a generous feast, have sexual intercourse with him, and then transform him into a pig and leave him in her pens. Odysseus and his crew landed on Aeaea, but Hermes, messenger of the Gods, appeared to the hero and warned him of the danger he was in, giving him a herb, moly, to protect him. By the time Odysseus had finished with Hermes and crossed the island to the palace, all his men had been transformed. Circe gave him the standard routine – she welcomed him in, served him a feast, had sex with him, and then attempted to turn him too into a pig. The moly cancelled her magic, however, and she realized that Odysseus was protected by the gods.

Circe decided to obey his demands, and freed all her captive sailors from her spell. They then celebrated with a proper party for everyone – and no pig transformations – that seemed to last one night, but in reality kept going for months. Odysseus and the freed

men stayed on with Circe on the island for seven years, during which time she had three sons by him. Eventually, a series of coincidences brought another of Odyssseus' sons, called Telemachus, to Aeaea. Circe married him, and he was granted immortality to match hers by the gods.

WORLD: The Greek myths are almost entirely set within a magical framework. The dividing line between the gods and mankind is extremely thin throughout them, and almost every tale features the supernatural. Unlike most mythologies, the Greek stories do not try to preach or set down religious lore, and they changed greatly over time, expanding and diversifying – more like an extended soap opera than a formal religion.

MAGIC: Circe's primary power lay in the ability to change a victim into another creature. She usually used a wand for this purpose, tapping the poor man with it. She also knew a wide variety of other spells and rituals, a legacy of her mother's power, but rarely made use of them – according to the major legends, anyway.

honourable Mentions

Many of the wizards of mythology, both good and bad, remain as anonymous or shadowy characters in the background who guide the plot of the myth or move it along. There are a number of important wizards in world myth that deserve to be recognized, though. **Odin**, the all-father of Norse myth, was a god, but he deserves credit for the way he sacrificed an eye and spent ten nights crucified on the World Tree to learn the power of the runes and gain the mighty magic they represented. **Baba Yaga** was an evil Russian sorceress who lived in a hut that walked around on huge hen's legs and was surrounded by a skull-topped fence. The skulls' eyes glowed in the dark. She rode around the countryside in a giant mortar, using her pestle as an oar. Her teeth were knives and she could turn victims into stone with a glance. **Dido** the sorceress travelled to the northern African coast and founded the city of Carthage. **Cormac MacAirt**, King of Ireland, was raised by wolves and owned a magic cup that would divine the truth. **Faust**, a medieval wizard, sold his soul to the devil in exchange for all the knowledge and experience on earth. **Kao Guojiu**, a sage, found the Daoist inspiration to become one of the legendary Eight Immortals. **Enumclaw** and **Kapoonis** feature in the myths of the northwestern American coast. They were twin wizards who tamed the spirits of fire and rock, and gained mighty powers. To keep the rest of the world safe, Father Sky snatched them off the face of the earth and made them into gods, of lightning and thunder respectively. Other characters – such as the ambitious and sorcerous Grand Vizier of Arabic legend, the evil Wizard of the Baron Munchausen stories who kept his soul in a nut, and the necromantic wizards and zombie-masters of Chinese folklore – are common visitors to the cycles of mythology. Every mythic system has countless wizards and sorcerers of different types and forms who appear in one or two tales and vanish again, but we do not have the room to discuss them here.

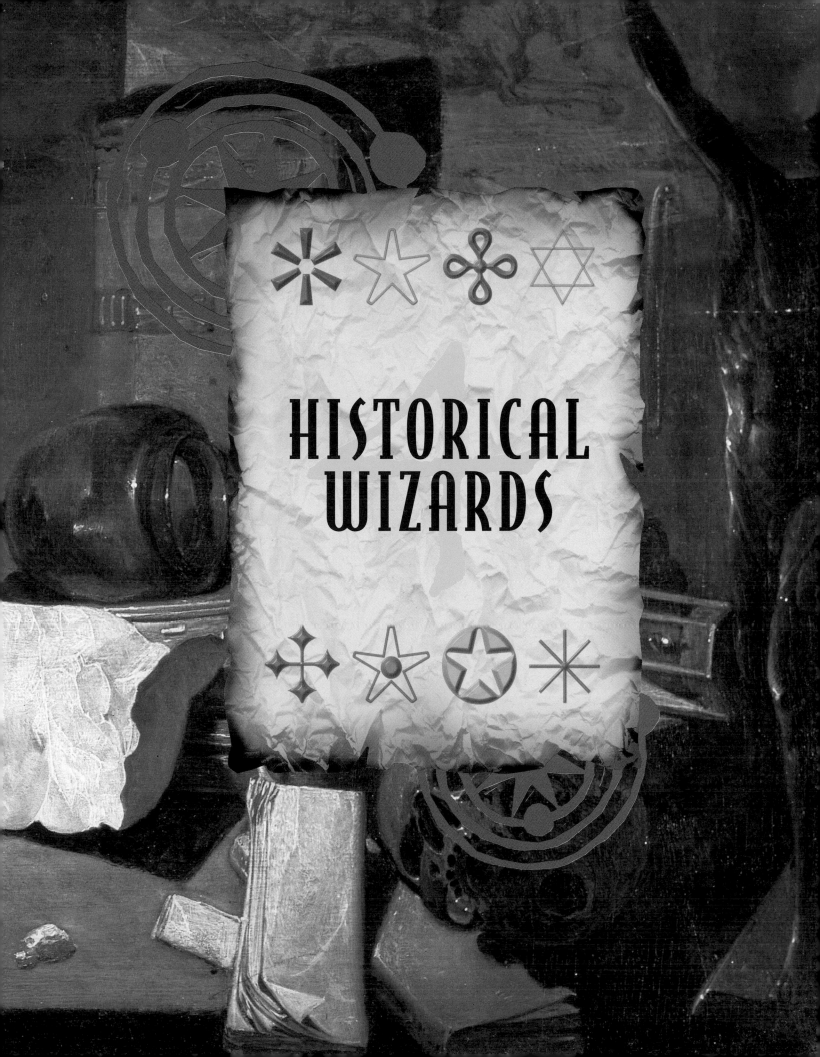

HISTORICAL WIZARDS

Down the centuries, the accusation of wizardry has blighted lives across the world. People have been tortured and killed on nothing more than a suggestion of arcane power, battles have been fought – and won or lost – because of it, and fortunes have been destroyed by it. The bottom line is that people the world over are scared of things that they do not understand, and anyone demonstrating uncanny abilities or knowledge is seen as a threat. The fear of inexplicable skills or powers is a constant factor in human history. Superstition, bigotry, jealousy and greed – all of these have made life extremely difficult for the groups and individuals that have been known for their rumoured wizardry. If there are any genuine wizards lurking in our world, they are well hidden – and, given the way that the rest of us have treated these historical cousins of theirs, you can understand why.

John Dee

One of the most notorious wizards in English history was the Tudor alchemist and court astrologer, Dr John Dee. He reached the height of his fame during the reign of Elizabeth I, and was known across Europe as a scientist, scholar and sorcerer. He enjoyed a period of considerable wealth and influence, but eventually fell from grace, and died nearly penniless. He left behind him a legacy of philosophical, wizardly, astrological and chemical writings and translations that remain important today.

BIOGRAPHY: John Dee was born in 1527 and educated at the Chantry School in Chelmsford. From there, he proceeded to Cambridge University and entered St John's College, before transferring to Trinity College. In 1547, aged 20, he made his first journey to Europe, and spent some time discussing a number of matters with assorted people in the various Dutch universities. The following year he travelled to the University of Leuven in Belgium, where he obtained his degree as a doctor.

In 1551, Dee obtained an introduction to the Court of King Edward VI, to whom he had already dedicated two of his books. He returned to court in 1553, when Mary Tudor gained the throne. By this time he was known as an astrologer, and was invited to prepare the Queen's natal horoscope for her. He also calculated a horoscope for the young Elizabeth, at that point still a princess.

Shortly after this time he began to experiment with magic. He quickly ended up in trouble, though, and was arrested on the testimony of a man called George Ferrys, who had accused Dee of cursing his children, killing one and blinding another. Other rumours accused Dee of trying to curse the Queen. His home was searched and he was brought to trial in front of the Secretary of State, but was cleared of all charges.

Astrology was a fascination that ran throughout society at the time, and anyone with a skill at casting horoscopes was in high demand. Dee's reputation ensured that his fame as an astrologer spread and he became quite a common figure at court.

When Elizabeth succeeded to the throne, her first commission for Dee was to name an auspicious day for her coronation. Shortly after she was crowned, she invited him to enter service in her retinue, and promised him a master's position at St Catherine's Hospital. On one occasion, when a wax effigy of the Queen was found lying in a prominent position outside a minor royal building with a large pin stuck through its chest, the general consensus was that someone was attempting to inflict disease or death upon the Queen. Dee was summoned, and his verdict was that it offered no danger to the Queen, which pleased her.

In 1570, Dee moved to the riverside London district of Mortlake, taking his library and research lab with him. The Queen occasionally stopped at his

 Right: Edward
Kelley invokes the dead
at Walton-Le-Dale.

 Background: Dee's
"Monas Hieroglyphia"
embodies the power
of the universe.

home to see his latest wonder or invention, and was said to be anxious for Dee to become her official court astrologer. He was an active alchemist at this time, and his search for the Philosopher's Stone may have had something to do with the Queen's eagerness to recruit him. He is said to have held discussions about the transmutation of metals with her in Westminster.

In 1581, Dee's wizardry really took off. He met up with a would-be medium and alchemist named Edward Kelley, who convinced him of his abilities. Kelley claimed to have found a pair of caskets containing mysterious red and white powders with which he was able to turn base metals into gold. Dee's diaries record Kelley using his powders to turn mercury into gold, and later pieces of brass, copper and other metal. This process is described as involving nothing more than adding Kelley's powders to the metal and then warming it in a fire.

Dee and Kelley travelled to Europe together to raise funds to work on the large-scale transmutation of base metals into gold. Although Dee returned to England in 1588, Kelley did not – he was imprisoned on and off by Emperor Rudolph of Prague, who wanted his secrets, and he died in 1595 after falling from a turret window whilst trying to escape. Queen Elizabeth, meanwhile, took pity on Dee's poverty and appointed him warden of the Collegiate Church in Manchester. Accusations of wizardry continued to harass him, however, and he had to defend himself further against accusations of devil worship and conjuring. He presented a petition to the James I on 5 June 1604, begging for a trial and exoneration to clear his name and to quieten the slanders that followed it. Dee died peacefully in 1608, aged 81, and was buried in Mortlake church, near his long-time home.

MAGIC: Although Queen Elizabeth's favour protected him to a certain extent, it was commonly said that Dee was a magician of dubious reputation. He openly practised the sorcerous art of divination, and held séances at which he claimed to raise spirits. His divination was conducted with the aid of an oval mirror made of black obsidian, which he claimed could conjure an image of a person into thin air. The mirror itself can now be found in the British Museum in London.

Dee's magical legacy has earned him a place of honour in modern occultism, too. In 1583, Dee and Kelley began a series of séance works with the black mirror. In this sequence of researches, Kelley entered a state of trance and worked with Dee to produce details of a special system of magic. This system, known now as Enochian magic, was based around the hierarchy of angels, their responsibilities, and their language, referred to as "Logaeth" (pronounced "Logah"). The Angelic spirits dictated several tables of letters to Kelley, along with instructions on how to use the tables to derive the names of all the various angelic spirits at all levels of authority. Specific words of Logaeth were dictated to Dee ("MRE", pronounced "Emm-Ree", meaning "with", for example), and letters were assigned numeric value, so that a word of a given numeric value was linked to all other words of the same value. This system of sorcery allowed for all manner of good spirits to be given sorcerous tasks to carry out on behalf of the wizard. Enochian magic is still practised by thousands of people world-wide today … with unverifiable results.

✦ Below: Dee's laboratory in the Powder Tower is still preserved.

Name: DR JOHN DEE

Time Period: 1527–1608

Region: England, with journeys into Europe

Description: "[he] wore a long beard and was of dignified presence…"

Dominant Supposed Abilities: Divination, invocation, transformation

Traits: Learned, inquisitive

Nature: Fairly good

Magical Power: Weak

Type: Ritualist

Domain: Demonology, alchemy

Goal: To acquire wisdom

Key Equipment: The black "shewstone" mirror, wax tablets for scrying engraved with magical figures, multicoloured Enochian Magic tables, Logaeth manuscripts

The Knights Templar

One of the most famous and controversial groups in early medieval history, the Templars rose from very humble beginnings to become one of the richest and most powerful sects in Europe. Initially founded to protect pilgrims journeying to the Holy Lands between crusades, they swiftly grew in both influence and wealth. At the height of their power, several countries owed them a lot of money. Their reputation was tarnished with accusations of wizardry, however, and they were subsequently destroyed.

Biography: In 1095AD, the forces of Christianity in Western Europe launched their great First Crusade to "reclaim" the holy land of Palestine from its Muslim residents. By the time the war ended four years later, the holy city of Jerusalem had been captured, and the united force of the Crusaders created the Kingdom of Jerusalem. In 1118, a group of nine French knights created a monastic order based in Jerusalem dedicated to forsaking wealth and offering protection to various pilgrims and religious worthies visiting the Holy Land from Europe. The order's full title was "The Poor Knights of Christ and of the Temple of Solomon", shortened to the Knights Templar.

The order's most powerful ally was St Bernard of Clairvaux, a Cistercian Abbot and the chief spokesman for the united powers and churches of European Christianity – so influential that he was often known as "The Second Pope". Bernard prepared the order's codes of conduct and oath of poverty, oversaw their formation and, when the time was right, sponsored the Templars for full acceptance within Christendom as a fully sanctioned monastic order. When they won acceptance, the Templars gained the full support of the Pope and the collected kings of Europe.

Because the individual Templars swore to poverty and gave all their goods and lands to the order, the group quickly became rich. Most of the members came from minor nobility, and had substantial wealth to begin with. This all went to the order, along with the generous donations received from the rich pilgrims that they escorted. After the Crusades, the order relocated back to Europe, and their wealth gave them power. Pope Innocent II declared that the Templars were exempt from all authority other than that of the Pope, which meant that they were above any earthly law. They used this immunity – and their great wealth – to lend money for interest, a practice that was commonly illegal. The Templars became a leading financial

✦ Right: A Templar fights a heathen enemy.

✦ Far Right: The death of Simon de Montfort, who had been the scourge of the Templars.

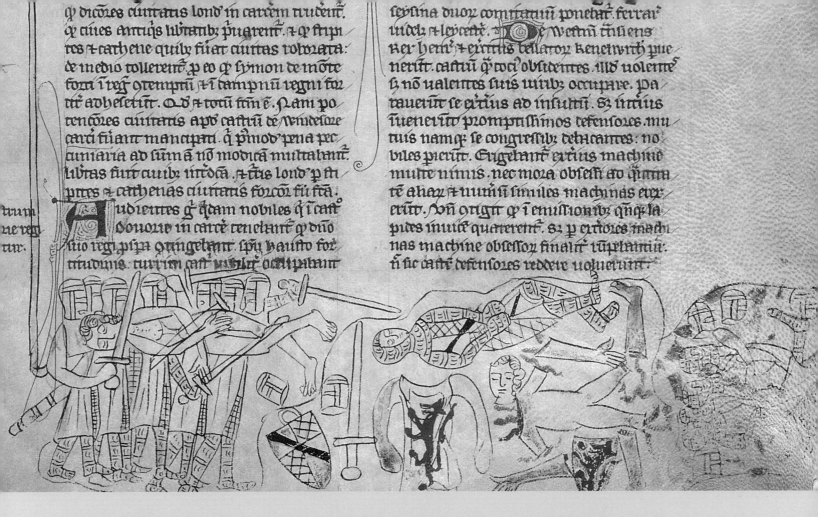

source for most of the European kings. In the process, they set up the structures and practices that later became the world's banking and finance industry, so now you know who to blame.

Almost from the outset, the Templars had been fairly secretive. They regularly held secret meetings, complete with rituals, at which the Order's business was discussed and decided. Exactly what went on remains uncertain, but people at the time were convinced that wizardry was involved. How else could the order's rise to power be explained? No nobleman wanted to believe that the Templars were simply better businessmen. By the start of the 14th century, the French crown owed vast debts to the Templars. The King, Philip the Fair – so-called for his hair, not his morals – conspired with the then Pope, Clement V. Clement resented the Templar influence, and the pair

agreed to destroy them. A rumour at the time claimed that Philip had received a vision from God that showed to him that the Templars would be responsible for the destruction of the Earth. There is no way to be sure, however, if Philip genuinely believed that he had seen such a sign.

On 13 October 1307, Philip ordered the arrest of all Templars on the charge of heresy, which fell under the authority of the Pope. This allowed him to take their money and torture them into confessions of their sorcery, which included worshipping demons, possessing occult powers, stamping on the cross, and performing illegal sexual acts. Clement V did his part by officially dissolving the order in 1312, removing their last shreds of protection.

MAGIC: Many of the Templars said, under interrogation, that they worshipped a disembodied head.

nchu. rrme

This was known as the "Skull of Sidon". Legends from the time say that there was a Templar knight who was deeply in love with a Moorish woman. She fell ill and died, and, overwhelmed with grief, the knight made love to her one last time. After he had finished, a strange voice spoke to him telling him to return to the spot in nine month's time to collect his son. When he did return at the appointed time, he discovered a strange, bearded head sitting on the leg-bones of the woman's corpse. The head spoke to him, and told the knight to take it with him. If he did so, the head promised to grant him all manner of good things and wisdoms.

The head became his guardian, and used its devil-ish powers to bring him everything that he wanted. In due course, he passed the head on to the order, and it in turn made sure of their success.

Other reports state that the Templars performed

rituals in honour of a strange being called Baphomet, which had the head and legs of a goat, and the body and arms of a lush young woman. It was even said that Baphomet sat in on some of these rituals in person, accepting the adulation of the knights. It is certainly true that the Templars favoured round temples to worship in rather than the usual cross-shaped Christian churches, and that their circular churches frequently featured lots of carvings of strange faces looking down on the congregation from the walls. A particularly fine example, still open to the public, is the Temple Church in the City of London. Not content with this odd style of church, the Templars redesigned the Christian cross for their own rituals, too.

It was certainly commonly believed that the Templars had all manner of wizardly powers, in partic-

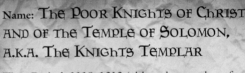

Name: The Poor Knights of Christ and of the Temple of Solomon, a.k.a. The Knights Templar

Time Period: 1118–1312 (although a number of people believe that some Templar groups survived in hiding and that they remain in existence today)

Region: Europe

Description: A religious order of warrior-knights who were thought to be wizards and sorcerers

Dominant Supposed Abilities: Divination, invocation

Traits: Rich, powerful, influential, bankers

Nature: Uncertain – they may have been innocent, and Philip's charges motivated purely by greed and jealousy

Magical Power: Fairly weak

Type: Ritualists

Domain: Demonology

Goal: To gain wealth and influence

Key Equipment: The Skull of Sidon, and, according to rumour, the Seal of Solomon, by which all demons could be commanded.

ular an ability to summon demons, predict the future, and curse enemies. One particularly interesting fact surrounds the execution of the last Grand Master of the Knights Templar. Jacques de Molay was burnt at the stake for sorcery on 19 March 1314. As he died, he cursed Philip the Fair and Clement V, saying that they would both join him in hell within the year. The Pope died just five weeks later, and Philip the Fair was dead by the end of November.

✦ Far left: Templars are put to death.

✦ Above: Jacques de Molay is burnt at the stake.

The Alchemists

Alchemy has long been thought of as a magical version of chemistry, in which muttering wizards cast brooding spells over crucibles and alembics in an attempt to discover the secrets of eternal life via the Fountain of Youth, and near-infinite wealth through a substance known as the Philosopher's Stone. Alchemists have been presumed to possess all sorts of different wizardly powers and abilities, even if they have so far failed to reach their ultimate goal. These arts have supposedly included talking with demons, brewing poisons and other dangerous potions, controlling the minds of others, predicting the future, and creating artificial life.

BIOGRAPHY/MAGIC: Despite the assumptions surrounding it, the art of alchemy has won the devoted research of hundreds of intelligent, well-educated people from all corners of the world for thousands of years. Looking at accounts of their lives, it is difficult to escape the conclusion that, despite the rumours, what the Alchemists were really after was the perfection of the human condition. They shared a common vision of humanity freed from disease and conflict, transmuted into the perfect likeness of divinity in a state of beauty and harmony. The ultimate subject of the alchemical transformation was not metal – it was the alchemist himself.

Alchemy as we know it was born in Egypt and was founded by an ancient Pharaoh, a sorcerer known to the Greeks as **Hermes Trismegistus**, literally: "The three times greatest messenger of the gods." He is thought to have lived around 1900BC, and was greatly renowned for his knowledge of the way that nature operated. Most of his works were destroyed at the command of the Roman emperor Diocletian in the third century AD. Of the surviving fragments of his books, the Tabula Smaragdina or "Emerald Tablet" is acknowledged to be the first and foremost

✦ Below: Roger Bacon balances elemental forces.

✦ Far Right: An alchemist at work.

D. TENIERS.

document to consider the art of alchemy.

The focus of alchemical research in the first millennium AD took place in the Arabian nations. Despite Diocletian's purge of ancient knowledge in 296AD, in which much irreplaceable material was destroyed, alchemy flourished. Alchemists such as **Zosimus the Panoplite** in the fourth century, **Morienus** of Alexandria in the fifth century, and the magician **Cedrennus** in the sixth century all left books, documents and records of their alchemical works and findings. In 750AD, Abou Moussah Djfar-al Sell, known as "**Geber**", or "Wise One", was born in Mesopotamia. He is generally held to be the greatest alchemist after Hermes Trismegistus and is said to have written over 500 documents, of which only three remain. He introduced several vital concepts to the art, and set the pattern of veiling alchemical works in allegory and mystery to protect the knowledge from profane eyes. It is his name that gives us the word "gibberish". Geber also recorded an Arabic version of some of the material in the legendary Emerald Tablet. **Rhasis**, a peer of Geber's, was an Arab who was famous for his practical displays of transforming base metals into gold.

Around the time of the Crusades, during the eleventh century, the main focus of alchemical research shifted from the Arabian countries to Spain, where the Moors had introduced it. A Spanish philosopher called **Artephius** wrote a book about immortality through alchemy in the twelfth century, claiming that he had lived for 1,000 years. As his time was coming to a close, he said the only thing he wanted was to give other scholars the chance to live as long as he had. By the thirteenth century, alchemists had spread all across Europe. **William de Loris, Alphonso**

✦ **Left:** An alchemist surrounded by his equipment.

★ Below: The successful alchemist must be at peace with the world.

the King of Castile, **Jean de Meung** and **Peter d'Apona** all left important books discussing and instructing on alchemy. D'Apona, a Paduan, was accused by the Inquisition of owning seven evil spirits, each one locked in a crystal jar, that taught him about art and science. He died on the rack. His friend, **Arnold de Villanova**, managed to escape execution, but his books were burned for the heretical suggestion that acts of faith and charity may be more acceptable to God than the Catholic Mass. **Roger Bacon**, born

in Somerset in 1214, is remembered as something of a medical, astronomical and scientific genius. He corrected the Julian calendar, discovered lensed glass (and invented spectacles), researched the telescope and predicted all sorts of much later inventions, such as steam ships, automobiles and planes. The ignorant said that he was a wizard in communication with devils, and he was imprisoned in 1279 and forced to foreswear science. He wrote only two or three alchemical works, but it is generally thought from his writings that he attained the Philosopher's Stone, and had to hide the fact to save his life.

Into the fourteenth century, many alchemists produced great volumes of work on the subject, often known at the time as "The Great Art" and "The Universal Science". **Albertus Magnus**, who died in 1314, gave up all his worldly possessions and wealth to study alchemy in a monastery. His pupil, **Aquinas**, spoke openly of their successes at transformation. The Majorcan **Lully** devoted himself to proving Muslim religion wrong and Christian doctrine right, and came to alchemy late in life. He found apparent success, and worked with King Edward II in England, transforming metal into gold to finance crusades against the Muslims he hated so much. Estimates say that he produced more than £50,000 worth of gold – an incredible feat. Edward, becoming greedy, tried to lock Lully up, but he escaped back to the Continent. Records suggest that he was eventually killed at the age of 150, by furious Asian Saracens whom he was trying to convert. Even at that age, he could apparently run and jump like a young man.

The legendary success of alchemists such as Lully caused problems through the fourteenth, fifteenth and sixteenth centuries, though. Charlatans, seeing the

★ Left: An alchemist performs a transformation.

Name: The Alchemists

Time Period: Technically 2000BC to the present day, but their heyday was 1100–1700AD

Region: Originally Arabia and Egypt, with a presence in China and Japan, but really mostly Europe

Description: An informal collection of men who dedicated their lives to researching the ability to turn ordinary metals into gold and silver

Dominant Supposed Abilities: Transformation

Traits: Scholarly, determined

Nature: Altruistic or greedy

Magical Power: Fairly weak

Type: Ritualists

Domain: Alchemy, naturally

Goal: To gain riches, immortality and the perfection of the soul

Key Equipment: A fortune's worth of laboratories, libraries, experimental powders and reagents, and other such material – alternatively, just the Philosopher's Stone, a crucible, and some lead

potential for good scams, conned all sorts of merchants and nobles out of gold and silver, for "research" or "multiplication". The problem got so bad that parliamentary acts and Papal decrees made the art punishable by death – even though **Pope John XXII** is said to have provided a lot of gold for the Vatican treasury by his mastery of it – and soon all alchemists were seen as fakes. Even clear, explicit, metallurgical treatises like those written by Isaac **Hollandus Sr** and **Jr**, a Dutch father and son, were ignored. **Sir George Ripley**, the Canon of Bridlington Cathedral, moved alchemy onto a spiritual domain, talking about the purification of the soul – but still provided gold for the Knights Hospitaller of St John with the aid of his Philosopher's Stone. **Thomas Charnock** claimed to have finally discovered the Stone himself, but not before his hair had become white with age.

★ Right: A well-stocked alchemical laboratory.

★ Far Right, Top: The boyish charms of the wickedest man alive: Aleister Crowley.

★ Far Right, Below: Nostradamus, who may have foreseen all, but if so he hid it a bit too well!

Thomas Vaughan, a Welsh alchemist, followed Ripley. In his book *Lumen de Lumine*, he focussed attention on physical, mental and spiritual reality. He also claimed to have created the Philosopher's Stone, saying at one point that he had to flee a foreign country when the purity of some silver he was trying to sell betrayed his skill as an alchemist; tales claim that he demonstrated his transformations, separately, to the kings of Bavaria and Prussia. **Alexander Seton**, a Scotsman, demonstrated his powers in almost ten different European countries before being imprisoned in Dresden for his knowledge. He was beaten, racked, burned, stabbed, and scalded with boiling lead, but refused to pass on his knowledge. He was finally rescued by a friend, but still would not pass the secret on. The famous alchemists **Michael Sendivogius, Botticher,** and **Paykull** all spent part of their lives in prison.

As the seventeenth and eighteenth centuries passed, interest in alchemy slowly gave way to other wondrous scholarly pursuits, such as the emerging sciences of chemistry, physics and medicine. **Jean Baptista Van Helmont**, who claimed to have touched the Philosopher's Stone, was also the first person to teach the chemistry of the human body. **Sigmund Richter**, who published an alchemical text in 1710, was a dedicated member of the Rosicrucian religion. **Helvetius**, a doctor, claimed to have had the power of the Philosopher's Stone demonstrated to him by a mysterious craftsman who came to visit him one afternoon. As science advanced, and understanding of the physical world grew, the idea of the transmutation of one metal into another became ever more unlikely and the alchemists, finally, passed into obscurity. If any of the few hardy souls still following the path have managed to create the Philosopher's Stone, their web sites are keeping very quiet on the matter.

Honourable Mentions

A number of important individuals have been noted for their reputations as occultists. Being an occultist is not quite the same thing as being a wizard – occultism draws on supposedly "real" magic rituals to influence events and people in a subtle manner. Science is fairly certain that there is nothing much in it. Whether it is science or the occult community that has it right, occultism has more in common with witchcraft than wizardry. Even so, it is worth mentioning a few of the mightiest seers, occult magicians, societies and other magical, real-world figures. **Aleisteir Crowley**, the self-styled "Great Beast 666" and "Wickedest Man Alive" was a subtle, intelligent and amoral occultist who was active in the first half of the twentieth century. He is widely regarded as the most powerful occult adept of modern times, a man claimed to be in touch with a number of spirits and demons, who was rumoured to have turned one of his acolytes into a camel, and who even founded

his own religion, called Thelema, which is still active today. Crowley first came to prominence in the **Golden Dawn**, an important British occult society from the turn of the twentieth century. **Michel de Nostradamus** is still famous for his series of obscure prophecies that seem to foretell the First and Second World Wars, the rise of the USA, and the collapse of our society in 2012. The **Etruscans**, situated in a coastal part of Italy, were renowned for being an entire nation of wizards, sorcerers and soothsayers. Their priests were said to be able to call down lightning in battle – that is until the Roman armies defeated and absorbed them. **James Murrell**, who lived in Essex in the nineteenth century, was known as "The Cunning Man" because of his supposed magical powers. **Michael Scot**, a nobleman from southern Scotland, was known in medieval times as a notorious demonologist. Accusations of wizardry have never been particularly difficult to come by …

P.E.PRACOWNIK

TOOLS OF THE TRADE

Wizardry is a complicated business. One requires a wide range of materials to be successful in the magical arts, and there is a whole range of items and pieces of equipment that the discerning wizard will never be seen without. In this chapter, we look at the physical objects that are traditionally associated with wizards. Not just what the various items are, but how and why they might be used, what sorts of variations you might encounter, and the sorts of magical properties that they themselves might possess.

Clothing

The first visible hint of a wizard's ability is normally the clothes that he is wearing. The traditional "uniform" of wizards all across the board consists of **long, baggy robes** that reach down to the ankles, topped off with a tall, pointy, wide-brimmed **hat**. If you want to tell the world that you are a wizard, robes and a hat are absolutely vital. The exact nature of the robes varies from individual to individual, though.

At the top end of the spectrum, glamorous wizards usually wear robes made of the most expensive materials, such as velvet or silk. These may be brightly patterned or plain, but tastefully understated **magical symbols** or runes are often worked into the design, usually in gold or silver thread. These mystical symbols are most commonly found along borders, seams and/or belts, but might also be patterned or tiled all over the robes. In some cases, the symbols have magic power themselves, and may be an important channel for the wizard's magical abilities. Particularly flashy wizards can have symbols that glow when they cast a spell or activate a magical power. Wearing certain sets of robes may be a specific requirement for the successful completion of a magical ritual.

Wizards who wear good quality clothing generally have tall, impressive hats. These are usually made from the same material as the robes, and follow the same physical and magical design patterns. Common colours for high-end wizardly clothing include black, midnight blue, gold, silver and dark green. Less commonly, good clothing can be made in bright colours – reds, blues, sea greens and yellows particularly – or might be in some abstract pattern, some of which seem to swirl and shift of their own accord. High-quality white robes are uncommon, and usually indicate that the wizard in question is evil.

At the other end of the scale, many powerful wizards choose to approach fashion from the bottom end of the market. Although robes remain standard, they tend to be fashioned from cheap, homespun wool or sackcloth fabrics, and range in colour from off-white, through various shades of greys and browns, to dull greens or blues at best. No robe of this sort is going to display magical symbols. Rather than the impressive pointed hats of their more ostentatious fellows, wizards of this kind may settle for a battered, **floppy hat** that looks as if it could have been tall and pointy at an early point in its career. Particularly die-hard wizards may do without the hat altogether, replacing it with a **cloth cowl**. These deep hoods may be built into the robes, but are more normally attached to stoles, which cover the shoulders and upper back and chest.

Wizards in this sort of clothing blend subtly into the population, and are free to roam around the countryside looking no more threatening than a harmless old vagabond. These characters are usually sorcerers or spell-casters rather than ritualists; ritual, by definition, requires all manner of objects and ingredients, and so does not suit travelling wizards very well.

✦ Far left: Circe uses her staff to good effect, turning Odysseus's men to swine.

✦ Below: A threadbare wizard.

✦ Background: Norse rune-masters preparing rune staves.

the wand and away from it in a straight line, so that the wizard has to be quite good at aiming the wand to achieve the best results.

On some occasions, the wizard may need to make certain gestures with the wand to activate the spell, perhaps sketching patterns or symbols in the air. Sometimes, gestures like these will leave behind visible strokes of light in the air, as if the tip of the wand were a marker pen that could write onto the fabric of reality itself.

In general, wands are no shorter than the length of a human hand, and no longer than a forearm. They usually taper slightly, from the thickness of a thumb at the base to less than the thickness of a little finger at the tip. They may be made out of almost anything. Although wood is a common choice, they may also be made from metal, bone, crystal or any other tough substance. Some are tipped with a **gem** or other precious stone, while others may have a metal or crystal **globe** set into the base. Many, though, have neither. Most wands are carved, engraved, burned or painted with designs, magical symbols or words of power, but some – mostly the wooden variety – are plain, and difficult to identify as magical. The traditional,

✱ Above: The spirit of a dead child is conjured by sword and wand.

88 ....Chapter Five

Wands

After a nice set of robes, the second most important piece of a wizard's equipment is a powerful **wand**. Unlike clothing, which is usually only there for display, a wand is a vital ingredient for a lot of wizardly magic.

Wands serve a number of purposes in casting a spell. They may act as a conduit, the channel through which the wizard's magic can reach the outside world. They may provide a focus, helping the wizard to concentrate on his magic and prepare his mind for the rigours of casting a spell. They are also extremely useful for targeting a spell – the magic often shoots down

✸ Opposite, Bottom: This medieval alchemist is down on his luck.

✸ Far Left: A wizard helps her client to gaze through a mirror and into the future.

✸ Left: The grinning demonic head of an invocational staff.

always made out of wood, as bones are rarely long enough, metal would weigh too much, and crystal is too fragile. They are less commonly decorated than wands, but may still bear mystical symbols, or be carved into various shapes and designs. Because most staffs are used for walking as well as for casting a spell, they tend to be tipped at both ends with metal "**shoes**". This stops the wood splitting on rocks and stones. These metal shoes are generally plain iron, but they can be made of more exotic substances and engraved with

stage-magician's straight black wand with a white tip is not really associated with wizards, except in occasional Hollywood movies.

Some wizards prefer a **staff** to a wand. Although they serve the same purposes, staffs are around head height, are as thick as your wrist, and do not taper. They are almost

magical designs. Some staffs have ornate headpieces rather than a shoe at the top, and these **headpieces** can be extremely large and impressive, particularly when the staff is being used in a ritual. However, although there is no real reason for it, the majority of wizard's staffs are pretty plain affairs.

Chapter Five

✦ Above: *Macbeth's witches around their cauldron.*

✦ Far Right: *A medieval book of spells.*

Cauldrons

An important piece of kit for any ritualist, the **cauldron** is much more than just a big pot. In ritual terms, a cauldron is a special vessel of transformation – things enter it in one form, and are removed from it in a different one. Usually this occurs as a result of heating, brewing or cooking ingredients. In the most typical use of a cauldron, a range of items and liquids are tipped into the vessel, it is heated for a period of time whilst spells and other ritual formulae are performed over it. At the end, a magical **potion** can be removed, either for immediate use or for later storage.

Cauldrons are more versatile than that, however. A good wizard can use a cauldron to turn all sorts of things into all sorts of other things. Typically, in the type of transformation associated with a cauldron, some quality or nature is added to the base ingredient. Water and herbs are turned into a magic substance when a potion is brewed, for example. In other cases, the symbolism is more obscure. Some stories tell of dead people being placed into cauldrons and coming out alive. Others refer to the cauldron almost as a source of rebirth – a normal person is placed within it, and exits it, a short time later, wiser and more powerful than before. There are also tales of a magical cauldron that could duplicate everything that was placed within it – you could put a gold coin into it, and take two out; put in two, and you would take out four. In a similar vein, some cauldrons are never-emptying, so that the food they produce, usually a bland broth or gruel, can feed an infinite number of people.

Some of the most sophisticated wizardly uses of cauldrons are associated with the transformation of energy. A few wizards, for example, have cast spells into an empty cauldron and made it come out of a different cauldron. Others have used the cauldron to apply a spell to a local area. For example, a wizard might cast a spell of water into the cauldron in order to create a huge thunderstorm, or he or she might heat the cauldron up to make an enemy army's weapons melt.

Cauldrons have also been used to distil incredibly large concepts down into consumable potions and **philtres** – the sum of all human knowledge, the knowledge of magical power, spiritual perfection, and so on. These are typically things that the wizard himself does not possess; somehow the use of the cauldron, through the appropriate ingredients and spells, can capture the essence of these concepts from the world, and simmer them down into something the wizard can use.

The ingredients that go into cauldrons vary wildly from wizard to wizard. Some potions require a range of mundane **herbs**, oils, waters and so on. Others are more exotic, and demand strange, noxious or **magical substances**, such as three hairs from the head of the King's bastard son, soil from a graveyard gathered under the light of the full moon, powdered unicorn horn stirred with a dragon's scale, or three ounces of sunbeams.

Whatever is going to be placed within it, a cauldron is a fairly standard item. They are usually black, made of iron, and shaped like a slightly squashed ball that's had the top cut off. A lip surrounds the opening at the top, to help prevent spillage onto the fire underneath. They have three or four legs, spaced symmetrically, so that a fire can be lit underneath them, and they also have a semi-circular handle that spans the top of the opening when lifted up, so that they can be hung up above a fire-pit if necessary. Most stand to about waist-height, but they can come in any size, from tiny ones you could hold in the palm of one hand to cauldrons big enough to fit in five or six people comfortably. They are hardly ever decorated. Both wizards and witches make extensive use of cauldrons.

Ritual Weaponry

There are a number of key tools that are frequently required during a magical ritual. They represent different elemental forces and qualities, and are known as elemental weapons, despite the fact that only one is actually any use in a fight.

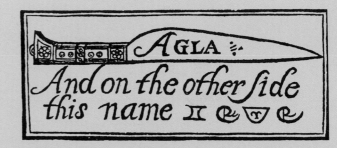

The **sword** represents the element of air, and, by association, is linked to the mind, knowledge, logical thinking, control and coldness. Ritual swords are used to compel certain types of behaviour or to tame unruly spirits, and to invoke mental skills and faculties. Ritual swords are often quite ornate and stylized. The blade is normally engraved with magic symbols, and the hilt is often complicated. The pommel may also hold a gem, crystal or special orb. Ritual swords have sharp blades, but despite this they are not usually much use in battle, as their weighting tends to be wrong, and the hit unwieldy.

Chalices, cups and **grails** represent the element of water. This is associated with emotions, feeling, psychic abilities, influence, transformation and love. In rituals, chalices are usually required to look into the future, the past or distant places, serve as a mini-cauldron by aiding in transformation, and can be used to influence the feelings of other people. Cups are, as the name suggests, shaped as simple, flat-bottomed beakers – in other words, there is just a flat base that separates the liquid in the cup from the surface that it is standing on. Chalices and grails are more advanced, with a round-bottomed liquid bowl supported by a stem. All three can be totally plain or extremely ornate, and are generally made of clay, pottery, wood, gold, silver or crystal.

Seals – mystic designs engraved in wax or stone, drawn onto parchment or on the floor, or made out of precious metals – are linked to the element of earth. They embody growth, fixing, channelling, linkage, protection and the shaping of power. In rituals, they are often used to specify the exact details of the results that the magic is supposed to produce. They may also be used to lock the wizard away from hostile forces or beings, or to increase the power of the ritual concerned. The most famous seal is also one of the most simple, the double-circle chalked onto a floor for wizards to stand within when casting spells. Others are considerably more sophisticated, if no more powerful – they may be created from exotic ingredients or with the aid of unusual equipment, specially prepared using elaborate rituals, or even devised through supernatural inspiration. They can appear as small parchment illustrations, pieces of ornate jewellery (generally gold, silver or platinum), designs scrawled on floors, or even as table surfaces, wall-hangings or obelisks.

✸ Above: A ritual knife to compel the element of earth.

✸ Below: The magical head of a Celtic sword.

Wands also double up as elemental weapons. They represent the element of fire, and therefore also energy, power, force and direction. They have already been detailed. A few other objects are also staples of ritual process, but do not necessarily embody a specific wizardly element. **Lamps** and lanterns embody wisdom and applied knowledge, guiding the wizard out of ignorance and safely to his destination. Ringing a **bell** indicates boundaries, beginnings and ends, and helps power to manifest itself – providing a climax to different stages of the ritual. Sources of flame, both indoor ones such as **candles** and braziers and large-scale conflagrations such as outdoor **bonfires**, provide a gateway between the worlds of flesh and spirit. There are plenty of other odd, assorted tools involved in ritual, but they are less ubiquitous. According to the famous fantasy author, Terry Pratchett, every wizard has at least one **stuffed alligator** hanging from the ceiling, too – but he's probably lying.

Tools of the Trade 93

Sacred Spaces

In addition to the various items of equipment commonly associated with ritual magic activity, most wizards require the versatility offered by entirely larger facilities. Many rituals and spells have to take place within some sort of specially consecrated area. The magic circle seal is a good example of the sort of sacred space which can be constructed almost anywhere at a moment's notice, but other types are less convenient. An **altar** is a vital requirement for a lot of ritualist wizards. At its simplest, an altar is a large block, generally made of wood or stone, on which different implements may be placed. Even these roughest representatives possess inherent power, though, gained either through specific enchantments and preparations, or just through repeated magical use down through the centuries.

✦ Far Right: A magician in his sacred temple.

✦ Below: Dee's famous wax tablet helped him contact good spirits.

More complex altars may include indentations to hold candles or incense burners, to provide a built-in bowl for fluids, or even guttering through the centre of the block to drain away the blood from a sacrifice. Others can include compartments beneath the main surface, either obvious or hidden, in which the wizard may store ritual equipment. Although plain-looking altars are quite common, they can also be extremely ornate. They may be made of expensive or unusual materials, such as marble, sheet slate, crystal, fired clay, or semi-precious stone. They might also be inlaid with precious metals, including gold, silver and bronze. Some are carved or worked into extremely fanciful shapes, decorated with carvings or figurines, painted with a range of abstract, religious or magical designs, or, if they belong to an evil wizard, inset with implements of restraint and torture, such as spikes and shackles. Altars may also form part of a larger **shrine** to a particular god, spirit or demon.

Sometimes though, an altar alone does not suffice. Some spells and rituals actually require a specific **temple**, or another special-purpose room, for the working of magic. Locations such as these have been painstakingly prepared for the purpose of casting a spell and have often been purified and empowered over weeks, months or even years of dedicated effort. It may be that the spell in question simply will not work if it is not cast within the temple, or that the temple plays an important part in modifying or controlling the

spell – or the forces and beings that it calls up.

Most good wizardly temples include an altar as part of the design, along with a complicated seal or other magic circle. The seal may be in the centre of the room as a focus for energies, or it may be around the altar, to offer protection and enhancement to the wizard. It may be drawn or painted onto the floor, but is more likely to be inlaid in metals. Temples are rarely subtle. Tall, flaming braziers often mark strategic points around the room's seal, but, if these are missing, burning brands may be set into the walls to provide light in their place. If the wizard habitually works with a specific god or spirit, the being will have a statue or other shrine near to the altar, which may also hold a lectern for a book. The walls will commonly be decorated with plush drapes, perhaps bearing magical symbols, and the floor may have mosaic designs. Doors are likely to be thick, with locks and a bar on the inside so that the wizard can make sure that there are no distractions.

In general, altars and temples seem to be associated more with evil wizards than with good ones. They are certainly linked with the idea of worship, because they are almost all associated with a particular being, or group of beings. The fact that the wizards that use them always seem to be evil may be some sort of comment on the nature of religion, particularly the worship of non-standard gods. Whatever the reasons, good wizards do not generally seem to have temples, and only a few use altars.

Laboratories

A must for the more experimentally inclined wizard, a magical **laboratory** is where the research for spells and alchemy take place. Laboratories tend to be concentrated into one room, usually big and rectangular. Labs are always kept out of the way of the rest of the building, partly for secrecy and partly in case something goes wrong. Many of them are in the basement, where noises and lights from experiments are going to be slightly subtler. Others are at the top of the structure, and have windows or panels in the roof so that the wizard can use direct sunlight and moonlight in his work. Labs usually have a plain, easy-to-sweep floor made of either stone or wood, with all manner of charts, diagrams, chalkboards and mirrors on the walls.

There are several items, naturally, without which a laboratory cannot possibly be considered to be complete. **Benches** are a must. Labs require all sorts of physical equipment, and that needs to be put somewhere, so most of them are crammed full with as many benches as the wizard can fit in there.

Alchemical apparatus is another staple. Even wizards who would never dream of trying to find the Philosopher's Stone are going to have flasks, pipes, retorts, beakers, burners, alembics, crucibles, dishes, jugs, fraction and distillation columns, bubblers, droppers, stands, taps, clamps and any number of other bits of glassware. This is traditionally all linked together by glass or rubber tubes in a series of tottering configurations, with various brightly coloured liquids slowly winding their way around the maze.

✦ Below: A well-stocked laboratory ...

✦ Right: ... and a more magically ordered one.

Clear **work-surfaces** are almost as important as benches of equipment, and the wizard may have a **dissecting slab**, a **reading stand** and a **writing desk** as well. A source of water is generally available. Truly flashy wizards may have large pieces of obscure **electrical equipment** humming and crackling away in the background, such as a Van Der Graff spark generator or a Jacob's Ladder, usually attached to dials, levers and big, chunky switches of the Frankenstein variety.

Less common may be a specially constructed **magical seal** for experimental spell-craft that keeps all assorted energies and magical mishaps locked within it. Some powerful wizards have large growth **vats** and tanks, made of crystal or metal, in which they create servants, reanimate the dead, combine living beings and otherwise tinker with life itself.

Locked **cabinets** turn out to be full of all sorts of specimens, ingredients, reagents and other interesting materials associated with the wizard's research.

It is extremely rare to find an ornately designed laboratory. Wizards who want an impressive lab almost always go for extra content, rather than decorated walls or inlaid magical sigils (seals).

LE QUADRUPLE **ORACLE** DES DAMES ET DES DEMOISELLES

PAUL BERNARDIN, LIBRAIRE-ÉDITEUR
53, QUAI DES GRANDS AUGUSTINS, 53

Libraries

Books play an extremely important role in wizardly life. Many of the greatest wizards developed their powers from the information contained in books, either right from the very start, or as part of a broader process of training and learning. Books embody knowledge, and knowledge is a wizard's stock in trade. From time to time, every wizard needs to refer to books for some purpose or other – learning a new spell, researching signs, portents or prophecies, verifying or recalling a specific piece of information, identifying a mysterious item, being or phenomenon, or otherwise checking something out. Because it is never possible to be sure what information you are going to need, most wizards hoard books compulsively, collecting as many as they can get their hands on, about almost any subject. That means that they quickly accumulate extensive **libraries**.

✦ Far Left: A French manual of magical spells and techniques.

✦ Left: Apollonius, Greek philosopher and magician.

There isn't an incredible amount you can do with a room full of books other than put them in bookcases. The construction of the bookcases and the room itself can vary, of course, and the number of books concerned will play a large part in determining layout, but in general most libraries are pretty similar. Small collections of books can be held in a study, where bookcases line the walls, and the room itself usually holds one or more comfortable chairs, and perhaps a writing desk. Larger collections, though, require the bookshelves to be standing free on the floors of the room or rooms, and the only real scope for variation lies in the contents of the books themselves. Prophecies, spells and rituals, monstrous and magical beings, spirit lore, superstition, history and scientific knowledge are the most common topics of books in wizardly libraries. Some libraries are incredibly grand affairs made out of marble, with carpet laid between the bookcases to soften the impact of the floor, while others are more modest, with wooden floorboards. They may take up one small area, or sprawl through every room of a castle, mansion or labyrinthine tunnel complex, but they are still libraries – and that means loud noises and naked flames are extremely unwelcome.

Magical
Societies

Magical Societies
Groups and Social Structures

Wizards rarely get on with each other. Partly, it seems to be the nature of the job. Most wizards need to spend long years in near-isolation learning the arts of magic, which must leave them with a number of social issues. The few, mostly sorcerers, who come by their powers by accident, often resent their abilities, and that resentment extends to other magical beings. But there are other factors to consider, too.

Groups and Social Structures

Wizards are extremely powerful compared to normal people. Often, only other wizards are able to pose a genuine threat to them – and it is difficult to relax around potentially threatening people. Wizards are competitive as well, keen to show off the results of all the hard work they have put in, or to demonstrate how great their natural talent is. That adds to the strain of associating with others. In other words, between their social difficulties, paranoia and professional jealousies, it is astonishing that any wizard even manages to be on the same continent as another without resorting to fireballs.

Some wizards, however, actually operate in groups, societies and organizations. These mostly exist to teach new wizards, but can also be formed for the purpose of achieving an important common goal, to provide each other with protection, or to provide a useful opportunity to trade techniques and equipment.

The Istari

J.R.R. Tolkien's masterwork *The Lord of the Rings* was the book that founded the modern genre of fantasy fiction. Its characters, locations, races and histories set the pattern for the revolution in fantasy fiction that followed, and it is still widely regarded as one of the greatest pieces of modern English literature. In a poll conducted by a major British newspaper towards the end of 1999, it was selected as the most important book of the twentieth century. Whether or not it deserves such praise, it is without doubt an extremely significant work, and the new film series based upon it looks certain to be a major blockbuster.

Tolkien saw his writing as an exercise in recording a fictitious history. The sheer detail he crammed into his work is astounding. This, as much as anything else, gives his writing its power. It also means that when he died, he left a great legacy of information about his world, commonly referred to as Middle Earth after the continent most of his tales are set upon.

✦ Far Left: Gandalf sits by a brook enjoying his own company.

✦ Below: Middle Earth – the ultimate hero of *The Lord of the Rings*.

········ Chapter Six

The greatest wizard of Middle Earth was Gandalf the Grey, discussed in detail in Chapter Two. He was one of a brotherhood of wizards known collectively as "Istari". They were of a race of good spirits, Maiar, who agreed to take on human form so that they could help the mortals of Middle Earth to overthrow Sauron, the most powerful evil force at liberty at that time.

The Istari left their realm in the west, and journeyed to Middle Earth in order to both support and coordinate the struggle against Sauron. The powers of good had long vowed not to interfere in the domain of the mortals, and this contribution was considered to be the maximum degree of acceptable intervention.

There were five Istari wizards, commonly named Saruman, Gandalf, Radagast, Pallando and Alatar. Saruman the White was the leader of the group, and largely dictated strategy. He was also the strongest of the Istari. Each wizard had extensive duties to undertake across the lands of Middle Earth, so they were widely dispersed and had little in the way of regular contact.

At the height of their influence, the western Istari formed the heart of the White Council, also known as "The Council of the Wise". This was a hybrid, strategic council that led the fight against Sauron, and was chiefly comprised of several of the Istari with various mortal leaders: Saruman, Gandalf and Radagast from the Istari, and Galadriel of Lothlorien, Elrond Halfelven, Cirdan, Deleborn, Gildor and Glorfindel from the mortals. Many of the elven members of the White Council possessed magic powers, but they were not classed as wizards in their own right.

The power that Sauron held, combined with the distractions and the powerful temptations of life amongst the mortals, led to the corruption of most of the Istari. Alatar and Pallando journeyed into the southern and eastern realms of Middle Earth with Saruman, but only he returned, and they dropped out of the chronicles of recorded history. Radagast became obsessed with the flora and fauna of the realm, and foreswore his quest in favour of dedicating himself to the study of the natural world. Saruman appeared to remain steadfast, but lusted after Sauron's power, and eventually he himself became evil. The leader of the White Council as well as of the Istari, Saruman used his authority to hide his corruption, and subverted the

Council by disguising his true intent as excessive caution. While the people of Middle Earth struggled to resist Sauron's forces against Saruman's delaying tactics, and the Council held meeting after meeting to try to work out how to progress, Saruman used the time to search for the One Ring, the magical item that would allow him to seize ultimate power.

Of the five Istari, Gandalf alone remained true to his calling. He was instrumental in Sauron's downfall, and also stripped Saruman of his power. With Sauron defeated and Saruman dead, Gandalf left Middle Earth and returned to the isles of the West. The once-mighty Istari brotherhood was reduced to just Radagast, with both Pallando and Alatar having shared uncertain fates.

In the final analysis, the Istari's loose structure seems to have been one of the main reasons for its collapse. Right from the outset, Pallando and Alatar apparently divorced themselves from Istari authority and abandoned their mission. With no requirement for regular meetings and with no central base of operations, the informality of the Istari brotherhood encouraged independent action, which undermined the wizards' cohesion. Lack of any clear oversight or

The ISTARI

Wizard	Colour	Fate
Gandalf	Grey	Vanquished evil and returned home
Saruman	White	Became evil and was slain
Radagast	Brown	Became diverted
Pallando	Blue	Missing
Alatar	Blue	Missing

✱ Far left: Gandalf stands at the gate ...

✱ Below: ... and at your bedside.

➥ Badger, lion, serpent and eagle, the house animals of Hogwarts School.

The Four Houses

House	Head	Colours	Animal	House Ghost
Gryffindor	Prof. McGonagall	Scarlet/Gold	Lion	Nearly Headless Nick
Hufflepuff	Prof. Sprout	Yellow/Black	Badger	The Fat Friar
Ravenclaw	Prof. Flitwick	Blue/Silver	Eagle	The Grey Lady
Slytherin	Prof. Snape	Green/Gold	Serpent	The Bloody Baron

Hogwarts Staff

Current Staff	Duties
Binns, Professor (deceased)	History of Magic
Dumbledore, Professor Albus	Headmaster
Filch, Mr Argus	Caretaker
Flitwick, Professor	Charms; Ravenclaw
Hagrid, Mr Rubeus	Care of Magical Creatures; Gamekeeper
Hooch, Madame	Flying; Quidditch
Lupin, Professor Remus	Defence against the Dark Arts
McGonagall, Professor Minerva	Transfiguration; Gryffindor; Deputy Headmistress
Pince, Madame	Librarian
Pomfrey, Madame Poppy	School Nurse
Sinistra, Professor	Astronomy
Snape, Professor Severus	Potions; Slytherin
Sprout, Professor	Herbology; Hufflepuff
Trelawney, Professor Sybil	Divination
Vector, Professor	Arithmancy

Former Staff	Duties
Grubbly-Plank, Professor	Care of Magical Creatures
Kettleburn, Professor	Care of Magical Creatures
Lockhart, Professor Gilderoy	Defence against the Dark Arts
Moody, Mr Alastor "Mad-Eye"	Defence against the Dark Arts
Quirrell, Professor	Defence against the Dark Arts

peer pressure allowed Saruman the leisure to become corrupted by power and Radagast to go native. Close scrutiny from fellow wizards is an important survival trait for any wizardly society.

Hogwarts School

In the world of the Harry Potter books, wizardry is surprisingly well structured. The collected wizards of Earth have their own complete culture, separate from the normal (muggle) world, and which comes with its own structure built into it. Quite a large percentage of the adult wizards in Britain seem to work for the

Ministry of Magic, a large government department that oversees all things magical. Others work for the wizarding bank, Gringotts, play in one of the professional Quidditch leagues, serve as journalists, or run their own small businesses, catering to their fellows. The tightest-knit group, however, are the collected teachers of Hogwarts School of Witchcraft and Wizardry.

Hogwarts was founded more than 1,000 years ago by four great wizards – Godric Gryffindor, Helga Hufflepuff, Rowena Ravenclaw, and Salazar Slytherin. Alarmed by the way that muggle people were reacting to the wizards of the time, the founders built the school – a sprawling castle set in extensive grounds – in such a way as to hide it from the world. Only a wizard can find it, it doesn't appears on maps, and mundane technology does not function within its walls. To normal people it looks like a trashed old ruin set in a patch of wasteland. The four founders had very dif-ferent ideas on what made a good student, and for several years after the founding, they each hand-picked their own students according to their preferences – Gryffindor preferred loyalty and bravery, Hufflepuff valued kindness and diligence, Ravenclaw wanted insight and intelligence, and Slytherin sought shrewdness and ambition. As the school grew, the founders divided the school into self-named houses embodying the virtues they preferred, and automated the process of selection by creating a magical Sorting Hat that would assess a child and assign him or her to the most appropriate house. The Sorting Hat is still in use today.

The four houses dominate the basic structure of Hogwarts. Each one has its own dormitory tower for pupils, complete with common room, bedrooms, and an animated painting that acts as the tower's guardian. The houses also have patron ghosts, specific symbols and colours, and are headed up by a member of staff, who is responsible for his or her pupils' well-being. Lessons are taught to collected house groups as well. The four houses compete at excellence throughout the year in a number of academic and sporting disciplines, attempting to outdo each other by earning House Points. The house with the greatest number of points at the end of the year is considered victorious, and holds the House Trophy for the following year.

Because the Sorting Hat actually makes allowances for a person's character when selecting their house, the four houses actually function as four small wizardly societies united under a single umbrella. Rivalry is common, and Slytherin and Gryffindor are particularly hostile to each other. The needs of the staff and pupils at the school are taken care of by a small battalion of house elves – magical creatures that live to cook, clean and do other mundane chores. Meals are taken collectively, in the grand dining hall. The castle itself is a warren-like building, crammed with the sort of secret passages, missing stairs, suits of armour and grand, sweeping staircases that can be expected in a school of magic.

At the heart of Hogwarts School is its immensely wise and powerful headmaster, Albus Dumbledore. He is personally responsible for recruiting the school staff, and the longer-serving members are all immensely loyal to him, despite an assortment of interpersonal differences. Dumbledore is widely regarded as the most powerful wizard alive, and is said to be the only living being that scares Lord Voldemort, the greatest of the Dark Wizards. Dumbledore has a skill for finding value in even the most unlikely characters, and employs a number of people considered dubious by the wizarding world at large –his judgement is usually proved sound.

The Jedi Council

Member	Rank	Species	Homeworld	Height	Speciality
Ki-Adi-Mundi	Knight	Cerean	Cerea	1.99m	Mind control
Eeth Koth	Master	Zabrak	Nar Shadda	1.91m	Physical resilience
Oppo Rancisis	Master	Unknown	Thisspias	1.93m	Tactics
Yaddle	Master	Unknown	Unknown	0.50m	Analysis
Adi Gallia	Master	Unknown	Corellia	1.67m	Politics
Yarael Poof	Master	Quermian	Quermia	2.24m	Illusions
Saesee Tiin	Master	Iktotchi	Iktotch	1.88m	Telepathy/ prediction
Even Piell	Master	Lannik	Lannik	0.70m	Combat
Depa Billaba	Master	Chalactan	Coruscant	1.64m	Insight
Mace Windu	Master	Human	Unknown	1.88m	Negotiation/ fairness
Yoda	Master	Unknown	Unknown	0.66m	Training
Plo Koon	Master	Kel Dor	Dorin	1.88m	Extrasensory perception

The Jedi

Basically serving as a wizardly police force during the days of their glory, the Jedi are a society united by their common goals and moral codes. Their purpose was to uphold law and justice within the old Republic in the Star Wars universe, and they did so with an impressive blend of wise

compassion and relentless fury. The ruling body of the Jedi, based in the Temple building on the Republic's capital city-planet, Coruscant, was the Jedi Council of the 12 greatest Jedi. The Council consisted of five permanent members on a lifetime membership, four long-term members who served until choosing to step down, and three limited-term members who had a specific time on the council. This mix of membership helped to ensure that the council remained balanced. With the Council keeping stable control, the Jedi were a powerful, united force.

Part of the long-lasting success of the Jedi lay in their training. Infants who were found to have potential for great strength within the Force, from which Jedi draw their powers, were recruited for training at a very early age. The implication is that very young children were separated from their family and friends before they were old enough to have formed very strong bonds, and raised compassionately within the Jedi order. The order itself therefore came to stand as both mother and father to its members, effectively bringing them into its family as a way of creating solid bonds of loyalty, obedience and affection. It is a technique that groups have used throughout human history.

The strong moral code of the Jedi further helped to keep the group together. The Jedi were the guardians of law and order, sent to arbitrate disputes, enforce Republic laws and catch serious criminals. Their powers gave them advantages far beyond those of more mundane police forces – they had the ability to influence minds, sense truths and perceive the past and future, all of which made it very difficult to deceive them or to hide from them. If a person was in the wrong, they would be found out and their crime would be dealt with appropriately. The strong sense of moral rightness that pervaded the entire Jedi order – that they were the exemplars of goodness and virtue – went a long way to blunting competitive disagreements between individuals. Jedi Council sanctions against disobedient or unruly members added a little overt encouragement for citizens to behave and to be nice to each other.

The final glue that kept the Jedi together came from the nature of the Force itself. The Force has two sides, wildly opposing poles of goodness and evil. These poles, the Light Side and the Dark Side, exert an attracting power on people who are attuned to the Force. It is impossible to remain neutral; any individual will be either drawn to the Light or to the Dark.

While a solid grounding in Jedi training ensured that all members were firmly settled within the Light side, it always remained possible to turn someone from one side to the other, snapping them from good to evil or vice-versa. The danger of indulging oneself in negative emotions and selfish desires was extremely real – being anti-social would pull a new Jedi towards the Dark Side, with disastrous results. Very few people are prepared to risk being egotistical, greedy or spiteful when they know that

being so may cost them their soul. With their very powers reinforcing their sense of moral superiority, their fear of disappointing their superiors, and their indoctrination from a very young age, the Jedi were an immensely disciplined and united force for good. In the end, of course, their discipline – and the self-assured complacency that it created – was turned against them.

Followers of the Dark Side of the Force, the Jedi's evil counterparts, are known as Sith. Evil wizards are notoriously bad at cooperating with each other, so it should come as no surprise to learn that there are only ever two Sith, Master and Apprentice. Their relationship is never solid, either; the Apprentice frequently plots to overthrow and replace the Master, even as the Master seeks to abuse and oppress the Apprentice. Even so, the power of the Dark Side can be seen in the way that the Sith managed to destroy the Jedi, who considerably outnumbered them, take over the Republic, and found the Empire.

Honourable Mentions

Even though they are the exception rather than the rule in the magical world, there are a number of other important wizardly societies. The **Unseen University** is the premier establishment for magical learning in Terry Pratchett's Discworld. Unlike the genteel civility of Hogwarts, however, Unseen University's wizards are a fractious bunch, full of petty dislikes and political undercurrents. Promotion of an underling within the university's structure has frequently been gained at the cost of the superior's life, and representatives of the different schools of the university have often resorted to killing each other. Despite the occasional outbursts of anarchy, though, the university seems to be now functioning well under the leadership of one of its strongest Chancellors for years, Mustrum Ridcully, who brooks very little nonsense amongst his staff. **The Academy of Tsurani** magicians on Kelewan in Raymond E. Feist's novels is another teaching institution, but, interestingly, it also serves to shackle wizards to a certain extent. They are taught that they have to work for the benefit of the Tsurani Empire without meddling in politics, and the Academy itself is compelled, under threat of military action, to enforce the Empire's will upon its individual members. In David Edding's *Belgariad*, the **Brotherhood of Sorcerers** is a genuinely cohesive collection of extremely powerful wizards, and their sorcerous foes, the Grolims, are equally structured – but both groups are quasi-religious, held together by their fight to promote the gods that they support. In the *Dying Earth* of Jack Vance, the **collected wizards of the 21st Aeon** – approximately the 210th Century AD – form something like a rather vicious social club, in which they gather to show off to each other, and go some small way to keeping each other in line through group and peer pressure. Despite these mild successes, though, the fact remains that wizards are more inclined to working alone than together.

★ Below: The usual chaos of Unseen University.

THE DARK SIDE

7

The Dark Side
The Evil Face of Wizardry

Wizards make excellent villains. They possess great power by virtue of their magical arts, so they already have a head start when it comes to ambition and control. It doesn't take much for the power that they hold to overwhelm their nobler side. In addition, the ways and needs of magic are frequently strange, so evil wizards are able to be cryptic, subtle or unsettlingly peculiar in a way that perhaps an evil warlord could not. Normal people tend to distrust wizards anyway, so alienation and resentment are common motivations. The overall result is that some of the most enduring evil characters have been wizards of great skill and power.

Darth Vader

Darth Vader is one of the most enduring evil characters of the past 30 years. Like several other characters from the first trilogy of Star Wars films, he captured the public imagination in a way that few characters have ever managed, and he is still an immediately recognizable, even iconic figure. His success is due to a number of elements. His physical presence was incredible – encased in black armour, standing over two metres tall, and constantly accompanied by the "urrrh-huhh" noise of his breather unit, he was like no character seen before. His voice, as characterized by the great James Earl Jones, was immensely threatening. Even his vicious, relentless nature made him captivating. He remains one of the greatest dark wizards we have seen to date.

BIOGRAPHY: Vader started life as Anakin Skywalker, a child of prophecy who is thought to have been the result of an immaculate conception on the part of the Force. He was born on the desert planet of Tatooine. His mother, Shmi, was a slave, and the boy Anakin inherited her lack of status. They were sold to a Toydarian junk-dealer named Watto while Anakin was still extremely young, and it was here that the boy learned a wide range of mechanical and technical skills. He was freed from his slavery by Jedi Master Qui-Gon Jinn following a wager on a race. Jinn recognized the young boy's potential and astonishingly high power in the Force, and took him back to the Jedi Temple on Coruscant for evaluation for training.

The Jedi Council could see Anakin's power, but their vision was clouded regarding his future. Sensing danger in him, they refused to train him. Following Jinn's death at the hands of the Sith Apprentice, Darth Maul, the Jedi Knight Obi-Wan Kenobi invoked an ancient privilege of the order to secure the right to train Anakin himself, as Jinn had wished.

Once he was inside the Jedi order, Anakin quickly became famous for his skill, power, recklessness and impatience – an uneasy blend for a Jedi. He had frequent nightmares, which Kenobi was unable to settle effectively. Finally, on a mission to find a missing Jedi, Anakin came up against an assassin, Ke Daiv. His repressed emotion surged out of him, and he unleashed

✱ Far Left: Morgan Le Fay prepares mischief.

✱ Below: Would you trust this boy with a used light sabre?

Right: ...and he
looked so innocent
when he was young.

his rage and frustration to kill the man. Once opened, these emotions proved impossible to control. Furious with Kenobi for the slow pace of his training, Anakin forced a duel with his master. Despite the power of the Dark Side within him, he lost the fight and was very severely wounded. Only his fury and outrage kept him alive. Various cybernetic enhancements were required to save his life, and the moment that the metal fused to his flesh, Anakin Skywalker became Darth Vader, and turned to the Sith.

As the Sith Master, Palpatine, seized political power within the Republic and began the chaotic revolution that would replace it with the Empire, Vader rose to power. He and his agents hunted down and killed the Jedi, with only a few – such as Kenobi, Yoda and Vima-Da-Boda – managing to escape the purge. Vader himself was particularly merciless, and personally slew many of the top Jedi.

Despite his prominence, Vader was not much of a politician. He tended to ignore affairs of state, preferring an active life in the Imperial armed forces. He also made good use of his excellent engineering skills, overseeing the design and initial construction of the Empire's most effective short-range spacecraft, the Sienar Fleet Systems T.I.E. Advanced Starfighter. Many Imperial navy officers bitterly resented Vader's privileges, considering them unearned. His management style did him no favours, either – his sudden fits of pique were feared throughout the fleet, and he was well known for slaughtering unfortunate, long-serving officers for petty mistakes. Unsuccessful assassination attempts did not lighten the Dark Lord's nature.

When the Rebel Alliance rose up against the Empire, out of the trampled ashes of the Republic, Vader was put in charge of the Super Star Destroyer "Executor", and tasked with suppressing it. He man-

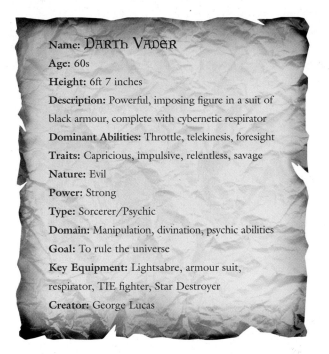

Name: DARTH VADER
Age: 60s
Height: 6ft 7 inches
Description: Powerful, imposing figure in a suit of black armour, complete with cybernetic respirator
Dominant Abilities: Throttle, telekinesis, foresight
Traits: Capricious, impulsive, relentless, savage
Nature: Evil
Power: Strong
Type: Sorcerer/Psychic
Domain: Manipulation, divination, psychic abilities
Goal: To rule the universe
Key Equipment: Lightsabre, armour suit, respirator, TIE fighter, Star Destroyer
Creator: George Lucas

aged to locate the rebel's headquarters, and finally killed his old master, Kenobi, in a duel. Vader was unable to finish the rebellion, however, because the space station that was to destroy the secret base was itself blown up before it could do so. This was achieved by the first of a new generation of Jedi, his long-hidden son, Luke Skywalker.

The rebels fled, and Vader followed, harrying them from hideout to hideout. Eager to stamp out any potential Jedi resurgence, Vader set a trap for Luke, but did not manage to capture him. Luke eventually returned to confront him again, and, following a titanic battle, managed to reawaken his compassion. Vader turned back to the Light Side and killed his Sith master, the Emperor, receiving mortal wounds in the process.

Vader/Skywalker died shortly afterwards, but having been redeemed by his son, he was able to take his place within the Force alongside his old friends.

WORLD: Vader lived in a period of anarchy and darkness that he himself was largely responsible for

creating. It could be suggested that his fall into evil was an inevitable result of his flawed training, but the potential for fear and impatience was always within him. The old Republic had been a stable force for order and justice for thousands of years, and although it was fairly corrupt, it was still largely benevolent. The Empire which replaced it was cruel and repressive, and this suited Vader perfectly. Within its auspices, he was not only free to indulge himself in the petty malice and bloodthirsty viciousness that he enjoyed, but he was actually rewarded for it.

MAGIC: Qui-Gon Jinn believed Anakin Skywalker to be the chosen one who would bring balance back to the Force, which he indeed was. Unfortunately for the Jedi, balance comprises of both Light and Dark. For millennia, the Sith – and the Dark Side of the Force –

had been weak and suppressed. Jinn fondly imagined that the chosen one would do away with the remaining corruption and cruelty, and usher in a golden period, but he was greatly mistaken as to the nature of balance. As the chosen one, Vader rebalanced the Force into a tool of both good and evil in equal measures. The Jedi paid for Vader's foolishness not only with their lives, but with the lives of billions of innocent people as the Republic crumbled. Vader typically relied on a relatively small number of his powers. His preferred technique for punishment – and persuasion, through fear – was a form of physical influence that closes a victim's airways, choking him to death. This was his favourite method of execution for his unfortunate subordinates. In battle, he preferred to focus on his superb combat skills and Force-boosted reflexes, calling on his telekinetic

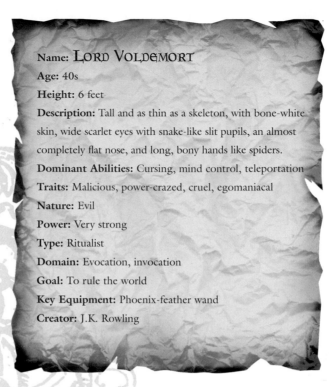

Name: LORD VOLDEMORT

Age: 40s

Height: 6 feet

Description: Tall and as thin as a skeleton, with bone-white skin, wide scarlet eyes with snake-like slit pupils, an almost completely flat nose, and long, bony hands like spiders.

Dominant Abilities: Cursing, mind control, teleportation

Traits: Malicious, power-crazed, cruel, egomaniacal

Nature: Evil

Power: Very strong

Type: Ritualist

Domain: Evocation, invocation

Goal: To rule the world

Key Equipment: Phoenix-feather wand

Creator: J.K. Rowling

✦ Far Left: King's Cross plays host to platform 9 ¼.

✦ Left: The chronicles of Voldemort's return.

powers to provide an edge where necessary. He could also sense individuals around him, read minds and, to a limited extent, foresee the future.

VOLDEMORT

It is said that a strong hero needs a strong enemy to bring out the best in him. If that is true, then Harry Potter is destined to become extremely strong indeed, because his arch-enemy, the evil wizard Lord Voldemort, is immensely powerful and very dangerous indeed. He is so terrifying to the rest of the wizarding world, in fact, that hardly anyone dares speak his name – referring to him as "You know who", in case saying "Voldemort" would bring them to his attention.

BIOGRAPHY: Tom Marvolo Riddle was the son of a witch and a normal muggle man. His mother did not reveal her true powers to her husband until after she was pregnant, and he promptly deserted her in disgust. She died in childbirth, leaving young Tom alone in the world. He grew up in a muggle orphanage, loathing every moment of it. He quickly came to hate his father, and all muggles by association. He swore that he would get his own back on his father for deserting him and for stranding him in the orphanage.

At the age of 11, Riddle was invited to enrol in Hogwarts School of Witchcraft and Wizardry, and he entered into House Slytherin.

During his time at Hogwarts, Riddle uncovered legends that the founder of House Slytherin had hidden a secret chamber inside the school which could only be opened by his descendant and spiritual heir. Riddle managed to gain access to the chamber and befriended the evil monster inside. He then used it to kill pupils at the school who had one or two muggle parents, known offensively as "mudbloods". When the school came close to being closed as a result of the killings, Riddle panicked thinking that he might have to leave and go back to the orphanage, and framed a fellow student, Rubeus Hagrid. Hagrid was expelled for letting a monster loose, and Riddle remained at the school.

Riddle hid his evil side and eventually graduated from Hogwarts at the top of his year, both well liked and respected. He promptly returned to his father's family home, a manor in the village of Little Hangleton, and murdered him. For good measure, he also killed his father's parents, who were living in the house. The method of death remains a mystery, although they were said to look as if they had died of sheer terror. Riddle framed the gardener – who was let off for lack of evidence – and left. His bloodlust wasn't diminished, though.

Riddle possessed great power and ability, and his openly anti-muggle stance won him a number of enthusiastic supporters amongst the traditionalist, pure blood wizard families. He took the name of Lord Voldemort, an anagram of his full name, and started gathering acolytes and followers, whom he named Death Eaters. He took control of a large number of other wizards by using a specific curse that gave him complete power over them. When he had built up a cadre of Death Eaters, he launched a terrorist campaign against mudbloods and muggle-friendly wizards in the wizarding world, and against muggles themselves out in the mundane world.

His ultimate aim was to seize power in the magical world. The Death Eaters' secrecy, brutality and power protected them, and Voldemort continued to grow in strength from the dark magics he was learning and the lives he was taking. More people flocked to his banner, some out of evil ambition and others out of fear and self-preservation. The wizarding security forces, shot through with spies and traitors, were powerless to apprehend the Dark Lord. Many wizards and muggles were murdered during the years of Voldemort's power, often in a spectacularly brutal fashion. The wizardly world was paralysed with terror.

Harry Potter proved to be Voldemort's downfall. For uncertain reasons, Voldemort was desperate to kill

the Potters. The infant Harry and his parents, James and Lily, went into hiding, assisted by Professor Dumbledore, but a supposed friend betrayed them. Voldemort tracked them down, killed James and Lily, and then turned his power on the baby. Something astonishing happened though; when Voldemort tried to kill Harry, his magic rebounded and he himself was blasted. Physically wrecked and stripped of his powers, Voldemort fled. His movement collapsed, and most of his Death Eaters were arrested and put into prison.

Although not many people know it yet, Voldemort is now fully restored, thanks to the actions of one of his old servants, a cowardly wizard named Peter Pettigrew. He has summoned his remaining Death Eaters to his side, and wants revenge on Harry, Dumbledore and the rest of the magical world. With his powers back at his command, he is in a strong position to attempt to obtain it.

WORLD: During the time of his power, Voldemort horrified the wizarding world. He had loyal agents (whether voluntary or involuntary) throughout the Ministry of Magic and other organizations, and was able to stay several steps ahead of his enemies. Effective opponents in the fight against him were murdered in their beds, or if they themselves were out of reach, their families and friends were slaughtered brutally. Muggle-friendly wizards were also killed, as almost anyone whom Voldemort took a dislike to could be. Most wizards were starting to view his victory as inevitable, because there seemed to be nothing that could be done to stop him. Fear and paranoia ruled the wizard community. Harry Potter's unwitting defeat of Voldemort guaranteed him immediate and ever-lasting fame.

MAGIC: Voldemort has a wide range of techniques at his disposal. His magic is both powerful and deadly, and he uses it without any pity or scruples. He is a particular master of the Avara Kedavara curse, which strikes an enemy dead and cannot be countered, and of the Imperius curse, which lets him control the mind and body of another person.

Another technique he frequently uses to instil fear is the Dark Mark, a symbol of a snake wrapped around a skull, which he is able to conjure to hang tens of feet high in the air over the site of an atrocity, to warn other wizards that he has done terrible things at that location. Voldemort is also a "Parselmouth", a wizard who is able to speak Parseltongue, the language of snakes.

MORGAN LE FAY

Once a student of Merlin, Morgan le Fay was a major enemy of King Arthur's rule in the court of Camelot. She was a sorceress and shape-changer, and her name indicates supernatural blood – "le Fay" means "the fairy", an indication that she was not completely of the mortal realm. She is first encountered in the tales that were penned early in the twelfth century by Bretonian minstrels in what is now France. Before she became part of the Arthurian cycle, she may have been a water nymph from Breton folklore. She is now a central part of the Arthurian cycle, the evil sorceress who helped seed King Arthur's downfall.

Biography: Morgan was a student (and perhaps lover) of Merlin, and learned a large amount of her magical skills from him over the course of their association. She is linked to various dark Celtic goddesses, and is characterized by her strong associations with winter, warfare and the harshness of nature. She ruled a castle near Edinburgh, which was populated by

Name: MORGAN LE FAY
Age: Varies
Height: Varies
Description: Beautiful woman with pale hair and soft, grey eyes, wearing an ivory-coloured gown and a golden circlet in her hair
Dominant Abilities: Illusion, shape-changing
Traits: Whimsical, capricious, spiteful
Nature: Evil
Power: Fairly strong
Type: Sorcerer
Domain: Evocation, transmutation
Goal: To bring about King Arthur's downfall
Key Equipment: Unknown
Creator: Unknown

✦ Below: Morgan Le Fay casts away the scabbard of Arthur's sword Excalibur.

MORGAN LE FAY CASTS AWAY THE SCABBARD

appear at Arthur's birth as good fairies, and give him a number of gifts that include strength, longevity and political power. The more commonly known Morgan, however, is a schemer and plotter who pushes the king towards destruction time and again. She is responsible for revealing the secret of Lancelot and Guinevere's affair to the collected knights of Camelot, for example. Having invited Lancelot to her home and attempted, unsuccessfully, to seduce him, she encourages him to paint a mural. His passion for Guinevere proves so strong that the secret of their love becomes obvious from the mural, which she shows to subsequent visitors as a way of causing trouble.

Morgan also played a part in the birth of Mordred, Arthur's son. In some tales she herself is the mother (and, as the daughter of Gorlois and Ygern of Cornwall, is also Arthur's half-sister), but more commonly she is just responsible for the boy's upbringing. She teaches him to disdain his father and trains him in the arts necessary to attack Camelot – ultimately successful, as Mordred fatally wounds Arthur. She also sends the Green Knight to challenge Camelot, frighten Guinevere and test both Arthur and Gawain, the son of King Lot of Orkney.

Paradoxically, although Morgan is King Arthur's enemy during his life, she becomes his guardian and healer in death. When he is fatally wounded by Mordred in the battle of Caemlyn, Morgan and her sisters arrive to take Arthur to Avalon in a magical boat. There, the legends say that he was healed, and he remains there still, waiting for the time when he will be called upon again in his country's greatest need.

WORLD: Morgan is best remembered now for the time she spent interacting with Arthur at Camelot. In many tales, she herself spent much time at the court, pretending to be just another beautiful innocent young

maidens, had wings which allowed her to fly, and could change her shape, in the manner of most Celtic wizards, into almost any other earthly form. She also ruled the island of Avalon, the blessed isle, where she dwelt with her eight sisters (also sorceresses), Cliton, Gliten, Glitonea, Mazoe, Modron, Moronoe, Thitis and Tyronoe. Her father, the old King of Avalon, had been Avallach, and Morgan may have had a consort on the isle for a time by the name of Gingamor.

In her very earliest forms, Morgan is not particularly evil. Although she tests people, she and her sisters woman, and using her guile to spread malicious rumours and cause other sorts of trouble. At other times, she stayed in Avalon and worked from there, or – particularly when she was bringing up Mordred – lived in the mortal world, secluded from the daily comings and goings of court.

MAGIC: A combination of natural fairy sorcery and Merlin's teachings in ritual gave Morgan a broad and powerful base for her magic. She specialized in enchantments and control of the weather, and spinning illusions and glamours to deceive and enchant. She assisted Mordred in battle by summoning a great fog that hid his armies, and her acts from Avalon show that paradoxically she must have had a great skill in healing. Like most shape-shifters, she seems to have been a largely changeable person, often performing very contradictory actions.

DISHONOURABLE MENTIONS

Regrettable as it is, there is no shortage of other evil wizards whose prominence and malice is such that they too deserve recognition for their dark ways. **Saruman the White**, in J.R.R. Tolkein's *The Lord of the Rings* series, is the head of the Council of the Wise, the leaders of the free races in Middle Earth. A spiritual being who has taken on a physical form in order to lead the fight against the evil Lord of Darkness, Sauron, Saruman ought to have been beyond reproach... Sadly, Saruman was obsessed with gaining the strength to rule Middle Earth as its tyrant. His greed, corruption and hidden evil nearly led to the utter destruction of the free races, and it was down to Gandalf, the most vigilant of the wizards, to strip him of his powers. Although he was allowed to live, Saruman's ingrained malice proved to be his downfall shortly thereafter, when he was brutally murdered by his traitorous follower, Wormtongue. Saruman had simply pushed the man too far. According to the non-fiction works of Andrew Collins, an evil wizard known as the **Black Alchemist** is not only real, but is alive and active in Europe today. His goals are unclear, but he is apparently able to corrupt the power of the land, set magical traps for psychic sensitives, summon (or create) spirits, and control the minds of others. Sometimes seen as a wizard, **Baron von Frankenstein** certainly managed to bring the dead back to life with the aid of his semi-alchemical techniques – and paid the price for his insane crimes against nature. Evil wizards, of course, feature anonymously in many stories. Plenty of them feature a maliciously unpleasant old sorcerer, bent and hunched over a staff or lurking in a hilltop castle and terrorizing the local population. These beings are often strange and frightening, and may keep their soul hidden in a foreign object, such as a stone or a nut. In one representative story, a Baron Munchausen tale, the evil wizard is holding a beautiful princess captive, and turns the heroes who try to save her into stone statues. A similar character can be found in a number of *Arabian Nights* tales, where the wizard is often a villainous **Grand Vizier**, the over-ambitious and frequently murderous assistant to the Caliph.